Yann Arthus-Bertrand Horses

Text by Jean-Louis Gouraud

with 202 photographs in full colour

This book is dedicated
to all the owners,
trainers, riders
and horsemen and women
– whether or not they
feature in this book –
who, together with their horses,
have given up their time
to share their great passion.
Y. A.-B.

For Utin-Royal, who has carried me
(and supported me) for so long.
J.-L. G.

Thames & Hudson

Contents

This book is not presented like a well-kept stable yard, with the horses contained in a neat row of boxes. It is more like a cavalcade, a headlong gallop, a fantasia of horses from around the world. The contents page and the index are designed to help you pick your way through the assortment of different breeds.

Foreword

Yann Arthus-Bertrand does not spend his entire life in helicopters taking aerial photographs of the Earth below, as his renowned best-seller *The Earth from the Air* would have us believe. He does touch down occasionally to ply his trade in a more conventional fashion on *terra firma*. In the 1990s, Yann became the first person to photograph ordinary animals such as cows, sheep, pigs, cats and dogs in a studio, against a plain background, paying great attention to details such as lighting and shade, and to finding the perfect pose to show off his subjects.

Yann always makes a point of attending the 'Salon de l'Agriculture' international agricultural show, which is held every March in Paris and brings together the finest examples of animals from France and around the world. For him, the event is rather like a pilgrimage: having set up his tent and all his equipment, including projectors, convectors and lighting reflectors, he lives, eats and sleeps on site, spending the entire week photographing some of the finest examples of the most magnificent breeds of animals. He has been doing this for almost twenty years and, as you can imagine, has learned a great deal about animals – and people – during this time.

However, one of his key discoveries has been the realization that horses really are unlike any other animal. Why do they seem more difficult to photograph? The beauty of a bull lies in its contained strength, whereas that of a cow or a sheep lies in its very placidity and therefore immobility. In the case of the horse, the opposite is true because its essence and beauty are revealed when it moves. This poses a problem for the photographer, who must portray that movement: how do you capture such beauty in a split second and fix it for eternity in a two-dimensional photographic image?

Yann's success at solving this problem not only bears testament to his skill as a photographer but also to his courage in deviating from the sacrosanct conventions of equestrian portraiture. The traditional shots are in profile, with the horse standing squarely on all four legs, front legs parallel, hind legs slightly offset, head held high (in order to be clearly visible and highlight the neck), and mane laid to the side away from the camera. Yann flouts all these rules. He does not want his photographs to resemble criminal 'mugshots' in police records, nor does he favour the clinical style of approach typified by stud managers' identification sheets. His aim is to show horses as they really are and highlight the qualities for which they are loved: lively, high-spirited, mettlesome, animated, prancing, supple and even ethereal creatures, a term that should appeal to a man who has spent hours in the sky in pursuit of his profession.

The photographs in this book are the result of fifteen years' work and several journeys around the world. Even though he took more than a thousand photographs – possibly even tens of thousands – it is still not an exhaustive collection. Nor does it claim to be an encyclopaedia or a technical reference. The idea was to compile a lovingly crafted atlas of the horse. Loving because this is a personal selection – Yann only included the photographs and horses that appealed to him, with scant regard for official or scientific criteria. He did not feel obliged to include any shots he did not like, a Barb here or a Nonius there, simply to give the impression that he was compiling a definitive catalogue. And he did not photograph a particular breed in order to appear well informed and above expert criticism.

Personally, I endorse this approach wholeheartedly. Even if he had wanted to, Yann would have been unable to produce a complete photographic catalogue of all the horse breeds in the world. Most horses (one hundred and sixty-seven million, according to the 1980s census) do not belong to clearly defined 'breeds' but to countless regional types, subdivided into an infinite number of local varieties. Moreover, there is a problem that has not been widely publicized, perhaps out of a sense of shame or sheer ignorance: the reality is that large numbers of breeds have unfortunately become 'redundant' and will probably die out altogether over the next few decades.

For instance, what do you do with the Don, the horse that was ridden by the Cossacks for at least two hundred years? It is neither fast enough for racing, nor powerful enough for jumping. It could be used for recreational purposes, but horse riding in southern Russia has had to take second place to the struggles of its people. This one example shows how closely the horse's destiny is linked to that of mankind. When you point out that the horse has been used and abused by man throughout history, many people reply – and rightly so – that, without human intervention and protection, the equine species would have died out long ago. Indeed, by creating and promoting the development of different types of 'breeds' with various aptitudes, man has fashioned the horse, if not in his own image, at least in accordance with his desires and needs.

The horse's intertwined existence with man appears to have escaped the notice of most of those who have turned the spotlight on the horse prior to Yann Arthus-Bertrand. In the text that accompanies the photographs, I have not so much tried to prove as to give examples of the way in which each breed is also a reflection of a culture and civilization. Just as Yann's photographs capture the movement of the horse in space, I have tried to place the horse within the context of time, by presenting his work in an order that – without being strictly chronological or rigidly geographical – does have a certain logic. I have attempted to show that, although the horse is now spread throughout the world, the majority of horses – both large and small* – are descended from those that lived in Eurasia, North Africa and the Orient.

This may be a vague, incomplete and unscientific approach, and one that is open to criticism, but it does not change the facts: the horse is a truly beautiful creature, and the stunning photographs of this gorgeous animal presented in this book really are second to none. I can see its creator fidgeting impatiently: like the horse, he needs to be continually active. He has other fish to fry, other horses to photograph and new shots to take. He is on the move again, somewhere between land and sky. According to an Arab legend, Allah created the horse from a handful of the South Wind. If that legend is true, he must have created Yann Arthus-Bertrand from a puff of smoke.

JEAN-LOUIS GOURAUD

* Many thanks to Alain Gouttman and Marion Scali,
who agreed to write the sections devoted to large horses and ponies.

Eurasia: birthplace of the horse

If any one place can be named as the origin of the horse and the scene of its early domestication, it has to be Eurasia. The vast expanses of the Steppes – stretching, broadly speaking, from Mongolia to Hungary – have seen the small prehistoric ancestor of the horse evolve into the animal we know today. Even if it is not known exactly when (perhaps four or five thousand years ago) or how man finally succeeded in domesticating this beautiful creature, it is almost certain that this important event took place to the north of the Black Sea, probably in present-day Ukraine.

Although surrounded by countless tales and legends, our history of the horse can begin with a few scientific facts. The Bible does not tell us whether there were horses in the Garden of Eden or on Noah's Ark, but we do know that the origin of the species dates back approximately seventy million years.

According to palaeontologists, the horse's early ancestors were creatures no bigger than a dog that lived on the continent of America, known appropriately enough as *Eohippus* (the 'dawn horse') and also as *Hyracotherium*. One day, around three to four million years ago, these small horses became dissatisfied with their homeland for some reason and began to move westwards, crossing the isthmus (later to become the Bering Strait) into Asia. They entered a vast stretch of land that suited them so well that they decided to stay there.

They flourished in the broad expanses of Eurasia, growing ever larger in size until they developed into the species known as *Equus* (the horse as we know it today), and the rest, as they say, is history.

In 1995, magnificent cave paintings, dating back to *c.* 30,000 BC, were discovered in the Chauvet Cave in the Ardèche region of southern France, which pinpointed the appearance of the horse in Western Europe to the Upper Palaeolithic era. They picture animals that look amazingly similar to the small wild horses described by Nikolay Mikhaylovich Przhevalsky (1839–88) during his third voyage in Central Asia (1879–80), on 'the harshest terrain in the Dzungarian desert', a region of Mongolia (now part of China) between the Altai and Tien Shan Mountains.

Called *takhi* by the Mongols, and *kertag* by the neighbouring Kyrgyz, this distant descendant of the prehistoric horse is now known as Przewalski's horse, after its discoverer. The present-day examples of Przewalski's horse, which can be seen in the majority of the world's zoos, have all been born and raised in captivity. Unfortunately, therefore, even if the attempts to return them to the wild in Mongolia and Europe one day prove successful, they can never again be described as truly wild horses. The last *takhis* and *tarpans* – their European counterparts, which lived wild without any interference from man – died out at the beginning of the twentieth century.

The three million horses spread throughout Mongolia – the only country in the world where horses outnumber humans – are not the direct descendants of Przewalski's horse as their cells do not carry the same number of chromosomes, but they are certainly related.

The principal quality required of a Mongolian pony is endurance. They are therefore selected by means of gruelling races over distances of up to 40 km (25 miles). The most spectacular are run each year in July, at the annual Naadam festival of the Three Games of Men that is now celebrated nationwide. In order to judge the ability of the horses, rather than the skill of the riders, they are ridden in the races by children – both girls and boys, and sometimes very young.

6 • A winning **Mongolian** and its proud owner Grubazar Baatartsogt.

10-11 • A **Mongolian** presented by Mr Enkhree and his seven-year-old son Bat-Erdenne, winners of a Naadam organized in September 2002 in the Khan Khenti region near Mongon Moor ('silver horse'), at an altitude of 1,800 m (5,905 ft).

Mongolian and Kyrgyz horses: one large family

Rarely more than 12.3–13.1 hh (130–135 cm), Mongolian horses are technically ponies. Small, stocky and 'strong-limbed', some people think they look coarse, or criticize them for lack of grace and finesse. One such critic was French writer and diplomat Saint-John Perse (1887–1975), who was not only a great poet – winning the Nobel Prize for Literature in 1960 – but also a fine horseman. In a letter to his mother in 1919, he described the Mongolians as 'misshapen offspring of the equine race' and 'large rat on wheels'.

However, even its staunchest critics are obliged to admit that the Mongolian's physical 'defects' are outweighed by some extraordinary qualities, and Saint-John Perse was no exception: 'On the credit side, one has to recognize a number of good qualities: robustness, endurance, sobriety and courage proceeding from an astonishing vitality that maintains in them a sort of gaiety, playfulness, and zest.'

As there is not a Mongolian breed as such but thousands of single types, it is impossible to generalize. The millions of horses in Mongolia may look very much the same, but they are all different, if only in the colour of their manes, tails and coats. In fact, the Mongols have more than five hundred terms to describe their horses' coats. This does not stop local breeders giving off mixed messages about these horses: some will tell you that a certain region is renowned for the quality of its horses, others that a specific valley produces particularly fast horses, but it is all rather vague and confused. At most, it is possible to distinguish certain differences between horses from the Gobi Desert and those from the Altai Mountains, for example, but it would be inappropriate to classify them as two distinct breeds.

The typically Western concept of a 'breed' was introduced only very recently into Central Asia, but dividing horses into categories and precise ethnic groups would be impossible here. How can you measure the degree of cross-breeding within populations of horses that have lived for centuries, and even millennia, in these vast, boundless expanses? How do you ascertain the purity of a 'breed' if you cannot guarantee its total isolation from other 'breeds'?

Although this is contrary to the Western penchant for classification, you simply have to accept the idea that the equine populations of most of Asia belong to the same huge family, whose branches and subdivisions stretch far beyond its region of origin. To the east, Mongolian horses can be found as far afield as Korea and north-eastern China (the historic region of Manchuria), to the north as far as Siberia, and to the west in Kyrgyzstan and Kazakhstan, Turkic-speaking neighbours of the Mongols.

Although they now have a tendency to lead a more sedentary lifestyle, the mountain-dwelling Kyrgyz people are still very attached to their traditions. One of these, hunting with eagles, was outlawed during the Communist era but has since been reinstated. Efforts are also being made to revive the local breed of horses, the pure-bred Kyrgyz, which Soviet zootechnicians corrupted by creating a 'new breed', the New Kyrgyz.

9 • The **Kyrgyz** horse *Kara Jorgo*, presented by proud owner Alymkul Obolbekov, with his eagle.

15 • The **Kyrgyz** horse *Jeerde*, ridden by Narguiza Kashkoroeva and held by her brother Toktobek Orozaliev, who is holding the hand of Narguiza's son Uchgun.

16, 17 • The **Kyrgyz** horse *Kyzyl*, ridden by At Almas Dosmanbetov.

Photographs on pages 9, 15, 16 and 17 were taken near the village of Barskoon, in the region of Jety Oguz (in the province of Issyk-Kul).

The Bashkirsky: fallen from grace

For many years, the peoples who emerged from the far reaches of the Asiatic Steppes, or descended from the impregnable ranges of the Tien Shan, Altai and Caucasus Mountains, have been grouped together under one name – the Tartars (or Tatars). This name has sent shivers down many a spine, evoking at once images of the Barbarian hordes and the mythological underworld of Tartarus, into which Zeus is said to have flung those who offended him.

The Mongolian-speaking Kalmycks (Buddhists) and the Turkic-speaking Kazakhs, Persian-speaking Tajiks and Caucasian-speaking Cherkess (Muslims) were all called 'Tartars' quite indiscriminately. The real Tartars were a dynamic, Turkic-speaking Muslim people whose spread was halted on the banks of the Volga, in 1552, by Ivan the Terrible (1530–84), the first Russian prince to bear the title of *tsar*.

In much the same way, the Russians have tended to group together the many different types of horses from the regions beyond the Volga and Don rivers under the vague term 'Steppe-type horse'. This naturally includes the Kyrgyz and Bashkirsky horses.

The Bashkirsky horses belong to a group that is ethnically, linguistically and religiously very similar to the neighbouring Tartars. Originally nomadic, they settled in the southern Urals in the tenth century, at the confluence of the Volga and its tributary the Kama. Here they developed a 'breed' of robust, docile and extremely adaptable horses, with an average height of 14.3 hh (150 cm). They must have been quite remarkable animals as they were used by the Cossacks of the Urals in the nineteenth century and inspired the great Russian novelist and moral philosopher Leo Tolstoy (1828–1910).

Tolstoy, a great horse lover, prided himself on his knowledge of farming and breeding, and owned several stud farms. On one of these, in the province of Samara, he crossed English horses and Russian trotters with the best Bashkirsky horses to create a new breed of saddle horse, intended for use as a cavalry horse. However, the count was a better writer than breeder and did not achieve the results he had hoped for. He finally abandoned the project and had to make do with ordinary horses for the daily excursions that constituted his favourite pastime until his death.

As for the Bashkirsky, it continued to perform tasks that, while they may have been less glorious, were certainly just as useful. Employed by the Bashkir herdsmen for riding, and as a harness or light draught animal, they were gradually relegated to the role of milk producers.

Koumiss – slightly fermented mare's milk and the traditional drink of the people of the Steppes – was rediscovered by Soviet scientists and upgraded to the status of a 'product beneficial to the health of working people'. As a region of cures and health resorts, the tiny Bashkir republic of Bashkortostan – a member of the Russian Federation, with Ufa as its capital – became one of the main regions for the production of this magic potion.

Although most of the *kolkhoz* (collective farms) specializing in the production of *koumiss* have now disappeared, a few private breeders perpetuate the tradition. A good mare, milked seven or eight times a day, can produce a daily yield of 3–4 litres (5–7 pints) of milk.

19 • The three-year-old **Bashkirsky** mare *Aïsseloy* (by *Sultan* out of *Aïssou*), winner of a gold medal (Kazan) and bronze medal (Saint Petersburg) in 2002, accompanied by the golden smile of Guennady Timofeyev.

21 • The **Bashkirsky** mare *Anessa*, born at the Ufa Stud Farm (1993) and winner of a gold medal (Kazan) and a silver medal (Moscow) in 2001, presented 'with foal at foot' by Grigori Arkadiev, a breeder from Olkhovoye. Her foal is held by Gulnar Gainodinova, who has a bucket of *koumiss* on her arm.

The majestic Akhal-Teke: a world apart

'Golden', 'the only pure-bred horse that is really pure', 'the most beautiful horse in the world' – it is impossible to describe the Akhal-Teke without using superlatives. It is a truly exceptional animal, as different from other horses as the greyhound is different from other dogs.

The Akhal-Teke is from Turkmenistan, a former Soviet Republic in Central Asia rich in vast natural gas reserves, which lies between the Caspian Sea and Afghanistan, bounded by Uzbekistan to the north and Iran to the south. The Akhal-Teke originated in the Akhal Valley, a prosperous oasis in the middle of the Karakum Desert. This paradise is the home of the Teke Turkmens, who are famous for the quality of their embroidery, jewelry and carpets.

However, the Teke Turkmens' greatest success is not a traditional craft product but a horse. Not particularly large, it stands between 15.3 and 16.1 hh (160–165 cm) and is slender, fine, graceful and aristocratic, with a silken coat that has a metallic bloom, and long, slender legs that give it 'plenty of air under its belly'. It has a soft, gliding and elastic stride, a high-set neck, an expressive head, and sometimes virtually no mane or forelock. It was described as 'a horse that commands respect' by Maria Cherkesova, a Russian national living in Ashgabat, and known as the 'mother of the Akhal-Teke' since she devoted her entire life (she died in 2003) to protecting this magnificent breed. It had become an endangered species under the combined threat of natural disasters (violent earthquakes in 1924 and 1948) and human crassness. Having decided that the horse should be replaced by machinery, in the 1950s the Soviet authorities decreed that the Akhal-Teke should be slaughtered for meat!

What a sorry end this would have been for such a magnificent animal, a horse with such a prestigious past. As far as the Turkmens are concerned, there is no doubt whatsoever that their horse, which today features in their national coat of arms, is the ancestor of all horses. They are quite convinced that the Scythians, the Parthians and even the Amazons were mounted on Akhal-Tekes; or, indeed, that Bucephalus, the legendary horse of Alexander the Great (356–323 BC), or the famous 'heavenly horses' of the emperors of China were also Akhal-Tekes.

The breed would probably have become extinct had it not been for the courage of dedicated specialists like Maria Cherkesova or the French-born Soviet zootechnician Vladimir Chamborant, who opposed its slaughter. With an estimated total world population of just over three thousand, the Akhal-Teke is a rare animal. Fortunately, many people today appreciate and value it, not only in its homeland but also in neighbouring countries (especially in European Russia), Germany and, more recently, the United States.

Highly prized for many years for its great endurance and stamina, the horse of the Turkmens has proved to be extremely adept at dressage. One of the top medal winners in the history of the Olympic Games was an indigenous Akhal-Teke from the famous Lugovsky Stud Farm, in Kazakhstan. *Absent* – whose name has sometimes been translated as *Absinthe* – won a gold medal at the Rome Olympics in 1960, and bronze medals in Tokyo (1964) and Mexico City (1968).

This aptitude for *haute école*, combined with its great beauty, has also made the Akhal-Teke much sought-after by circuses throughout the world.

The Orlov trotter: the count's finest creation

'In the mid-eighteenth century, there were no good carriage horses in Russia, even though there was an obvious need for them as this was the only possible means of transport within such a vast country. The Steppe-type horses, although excellent saddle horses, were often too small, while European horses did not have enough stamina over long distances.' This was how eminent Soviet horse expert Igor Bobilev – professor of veterinary medicine and, until his death in December 2000, the permanent representative of the USSR and then Russia on the Fédération Équestre Internationale (International Equestrian Federation) – explained his country's determined attempts to create various types of light draught horse.

The most successful and most beautiful of these was produced by Count Aleksey Grigoryevich Orlov (1737–1808). His conduct may have been reprehensible at times – he may even have been behind the assassination of the Emperor Peter III (1728–62), which enabled Catherine the Great (1729–96) to become Empress – but he was a brilliant horse breeder. He built the magnificent Khrenovsky Stud on the broad expanses of pasture land in the Voronezh region, given to him by the grateful Empress, about 500 km (310 miles) south of Moscow. Here, by skilfully crossing Arab, Danish, Dutch and English blood, he created the Orlov trotter, a breed of powerful and fast-moving horses.

This new breed was a great success. Of average height – about 15.3 hh (160 cm) – with a roomy chest, strong loins and hard legs, for over two hundred years it has proved ideal for pulling the many types of carriages that travel the length and breadth of Russia. No self-respecting *troïka* would have anything other than an Orlov between the shafts. The Orlov trotter, usually dapple grey, even became something of a national symbol – so much so that, thirty years after the count's death, Emperor Nicholas I (1796–1855) decided to 'nationalize' the Khrenovsky Stud, which is still breeding Orlov trotters today.

24, 25, 27 • *Murgi*, an **Akhal-Teke** stallion born in 2000 (by *Gayaz* out of *Almagul*),
at the Chamborant Stud Farm in the region of Vladimir, near Moscow.

28 • The **Orlov trotter** mare *Pika* (by *Quartet* out of *Pepa*), from the Khrenovsky Stud,
held by the director of Russian National Stud Farms Alexander Timchenko.

**Count Orlov also helped to create a breed of Russian riding horse which,
combined with the horses produced on the stud farm of another enthusiast,
Count Rostopchin, gave rise to a breed of very elegant black horses: the
Orlov-Rostopchin. After almost dying out during the Communist era, the breed
is once again being promoted by the Russian government, especially at the
Starojilov National Stud, about 250 km (155 miles) south-east of Moscow.**

29 • *Indikator*, a four-year-old **Orlov-Rostopchin** (by *Intrigan* out of *Delyana*),
held by Maria Pozhilkova.

Heavy and light draught horses: enjoying the limelight

Russia has had a plentiful supply of saddle horses, descended from the 'breeds' created by the nomads of the Steppes of Central Asia and the warrior-herdsmen of the Caucasus Mountains. However, it has always found it more difficult to develop animals well suited to agricultural and heavy draught work.

Peter the Great (1672–1725) had encouraged the creation of a type of draught horse known as the Bityug (or Bitjug), crossing imported Dutch stallions with mares from the Voronezh region, but results proved disappointing. It was not until the mid–twentieth century that more satisfactory results were achieved with the Vladimir Heavy Draught and the Russian Heavy Draught. The former, at 16.1 hh (165 cm) and about 760 kg (1,675 lb), was developed in the 1940s using French (Percheron), Belgian (Ardennais) and Scottish (Clydesdale) stallions. The 15.3 hh (160 cm) Russian Heavy Draught, built by crossing Brabant stallions with Russian mares, carries more weight (780 kg or 1,720 lb) and was officially registered as a distinct breed in 1952.

31 • The **Vladimir Heavy Draught** mare *Galatea*, born in 1988 at the Yuriev-Polsky Stud Farm (in the region of Vladimir) and descended from a long line of breed champions, lovingly presented by Slava Kiceliov.

32 • The **Russian Heavy Draught** stallion *Jar*, born in 1991 at the Mordova Stud Farm and breed champion in 1996.

33 • The **Russian Heavy Draught** stallion *Kourière*, born in 1998 at the Pochinkovsky Stud Farm, presented by Alexander Morozov.

34, 35 • *Pingouin*, a **Belorussian Draught** (a light draught horse from Belarus) born in 1991, presented by his handler Andrei Letunov.

The Kabardin and Karachai: legends of the Caucasus

The Caucasus is a land of legend. Famed for its beautiful women, it appears to have been a favourite source of concubines for the Ottoman sultans. It is also renowned for the unusually high number of centenarians. The region is an incredible melting pot of many different ethnic groups and an assortment of totally unconnected languages, which bear no resemblance to one another and are totally incomprehensible from one valley to the next. The Chechens do not understand the Cherkess, who do not understand the Ossetes, and so on.

There is, of course, a legend that explains this strange phenomenon. Some time after God had created mankind, He realized that something was wrong: He had forgotten to give them language. So He hurriedly piled a number of different languages into His heavenly chariot and began distributing them around the world. When He reached the Caucasus, one of the chariot wheels hit Mount Elbrus which, at 5,633 m (18,480 ft), is the highest peak in the Caucasus Mountains. The chariot jolted so violently that a pile of languages slipped through the slatted sides and fell to Earth. Having made sure He had enough languages to complete His task, God decided to leave them where they had fallen.

Another legend links the region's horses to the creation of the Caucasus Mountains. Long, long ago, it was said that the mountains had the power to move. One day, as they travelled between the Caspian and Black Seas, they saw herds of splendid wild horses. These horses were so magnificent that the mountains were rooted to the spot for eternity, forming the Caucasus Mountains.

There is an element of truth in this legend, in that the vast plains on the foothills of the Caucasus Mountains provide grazing for an amazing variety of horses. The Russians have established a number of stud farms here, some of which have become internationally renowned. One example is the Tersk Stud, founded in 1889 by Count Alexei Stroganov on the outskirts of the delightful spa town of Pyatigorsk ('Five Mountains'), which was popular in summer with Muscovite high society. Today, Tersk is one of the most prestigious stud farms in the world for the production of pure-bred Arabs. A few miles away, the Stavropol Stud produces the best Akhal-Tekes bred outside their region of origin, as well as excellent Terskys, which – as their name suggests – were first developed on the Tersk Stud. Terskys are small grey horses with a strong Arab influence, but much more affordable.

On the vast expanses of the northern Caucasus, the Soviet regime also perpetuated the tradition by creating several top-quality state stud farms between the cities of Stavropol and Krasnodar. In 1920, they founded the Voskod ('dawn') Stud, which produced some of the best English Thoroughbreds in the USSR, including the famous champion *Aniline*. In the 1960s, a stud farm for sporting horses (especially Trakehners) was set up within the *sovkhoz* (state farm) model. It was not only much admired by great *apparatchiks* such as Nikita Sergeyevich Khrushchev (1894–1971) and Leonid Ilyich Brezhnev (1906–82), who visited the stud, but also by specialists, including Olympic dressage champion and silver medallist Elena Petushkova.

Arabs, English Thoroughbreds and Turkomans, the breeds raised so successfully in the northern Caucasus, are obviously not indigenous to the region. The real Caucasian horses are found in the mountains, in the small republics bordering Georgia, where the herdsmen still (although probably not for much longer) use horses to round up their flocks of goats and sheep. It is here, deep in the mountains around Mount Elbrus, that you will find the pearl of the Caucasus: the Kabardin. According to yet another legend, this horse is the perfect product of centuries of inter-breeding between all the breeds of the region, as well as those brought in during numerous invasions. The Kabardin is said to combine all the qualities but none of the defects of the breeds that have produced it. Although in reality it may not possess all the qualities of its constituent breeds, it certainly has a great many. Sturdily built and usually standing at about 14.3 hh (150 cm), its slightly Roman nose and bay, dark-brown or black coat give it an air of elegance. It stands squarely on strong, well-positioned legs, and has a roomy chest and short croup, which makes it an excellent pack and saddle animal. The mountain dwellers of the Caucasus have always used it for both purposes and, before the advent of motor vehicles, it was the equine equivalent of the jeep.

Born and bred in the mountains – at an altitude of between 2,500 and 3,500 m (8,200–11,480 ft) – it has the respiratory and vascular systems of an equine athlete, which, combined with its hard legs and feet, make it an indefatigable climber. Calm, hardy and courageous, able to withstand wide variations in temperature, and extremely sure-footed, the Kabardin was once much sought-after by the Cossacks of the Terek and Kuban rivers. These days, for many people, this beautiful animal no longer serves any 'useful' purpose and is in danger of disappearing forever. However, given the chance, it would undoubtedly do well in the field of endurance riding.

The Karachai, of similar size and colouring, is closely related to the Kabardin and shares the same characteristics and qualities. In fact, the only real difference is its name, derived from the tiny republic in which it is bred: whereas the Kabardin is bred in the republic of Kabardino-Balkarskaya, the Karachai is bred in Karachayevo-Cherkessaya.

39 • The **Kabardin** stallion *Djenal*, born in 1999 at the Nalchik Stud Farm, held by Azamat Khazimov.

40–41 • The **Karachai** stallion *Paruss*, born in 1995 and the pride of an equestrian centre near Borodino, about 100 km (62 miles) west of Moscow, ridden by Ruslan Liskanich.

Barbary: a centre for world expansion

Another place from which some breeds of horse are said to have originated is Barbary, a former region of North Africa that stretched from western Egypt to the Atlantic coast. It was from here that the Barb horses of the Berbers spread southwards, giving rise to most of the African 'breeds', and northwards, where they contributed to the creation of the Spanish and Portuguese breeds. Taken across the Atlantic by the Conquistadors, these horses were also introduced to the Americas. It makes quite a history and it does not end there: Barb blood is also present in the English Thoroughbred, the Neapolitan, the Lipizzaner and the Friesian.

The horse has existed in Africa for thousands of years, as its depiction in the Tassili rock paintings at Tassili n'Ajjer in southern Algeria proves. Of the thousands of engravings and paintings discovered there in the 1950s by French ethnologist Henri Lhote, the earliest date from 5000 BC. For Lhote, there was no doubt that the first horses to arrive on the continent of Africa came from the distant lands of Eurasia.

This is thought to have occurred twenty-five thousand years ago, during the last Ice Age, when vast numbers of animals migrated southwards to escape the cold. These animals included wild horses – or rather, according to certain experts, onagers (a Persian variety of wild ass) and even quaggas, with their sandy-brown coats and zebra-like stripes, but Equidae nonetheless. They are believed to have reached Africa via Central Asia and the Near East, only to die out during the Neolithic Age, *c.* 5000 BC.

It was only much later, in *c.* 1200 BC, that the mysterious invaders known as the 'Sea Peoples' arrived from Asia or Europe (their origins are uncertain) accompanied by domesticated horses, including some in harness as depicted in the Tassili rock paintings. It is quite likely that these warriors mixed with the indigenous population to form the people known today as the Berbers. It is also quite possible that

their horses were the ancestors of the modern Barb 'breed'.

Whatever the case, we do know that the horses used a thousand years later by the great Carthaginian general Hannibal (247–183 BC) in his campaign against Rome were the ancestors of the horses found in North Africa today. The horses depicted in mosaics discovered in Carthage (in modern-day Tunisia) – at about 15.1 hh (155 cm), with a strong head, a slightly Roman nose, short loins, and small, hard feet – leave little room for doubt.

Such continuity is extremely rare in the history of the horse. Those who praise a particular breed or breeds are often obliged to turn to legend and fable to trace their supposed origins. The Barb's history can be traced, with little need for embellishment, over a period of two thousand years.

About one thousand years after the death of Hannibal, the Muslims used the same type of horses to invade Spain and part of Mediterranean Europe; and a thousand years after that, the same type were again encountered, this time by the French when they turned the tables and invaded Algeria. In 1847, General Oudinot (1767–1847), a French marshal during the Napoleonic Wars, described the Barb as 'docile, calm, swift, patient, agile and indefatigable, combining the greatest

number of qualities required by fighting men'. The French army adopted the Barb immediately, using them primarily as mounts for the famous *spahi* regiments, the French army's native cavalry corps. One hundred and fifty years later, modern tourists visiting North Africa (especially Morocco) are able to admire these same horses in the spectacular and incredibly noisy *fantasias* (equestrian displays).

Although confined to their homeland for many years, the breeding of Barb horses is now gaining a foothold in Europe. The great qualities of this little horse 'with a sound temperament and strong back' are being rediscovered, especially in outdoor disciplines such as endurance riding and eco-tourism.

From the Maghreb to the Sudan: military stalwarts

On 14 June 1830, Charles X (1757–1836) of France sent an expeditionary force of thirty-eight thousand troops and four thousand horses to Algeria. It was a 'punitive' expedition against Algeria, initiated on the pretext that the Dey of Algiers had insulted a French ambassador.

The occupying army soon realized that these four thousand large French horses were totally unsuited to the climate and terrain of North Africa, and replaced them with the local Barb horses. In October of that year, General Clauzel (1772–1842), commander-in-chief of the expeditionary force, decided to create a native cavalry regiment that became known as the *spahis*.

Thirteen years later, when France wanted to strengthen its presence in Africa, the governor of Senegal, Commander Bouët-Willaumez was authorized to 'borrow' some of these famous *spahis* from his colleague in Algeria.

On 6 February 1843, twenty-six 'Algerian' cavalrymen (half were European, half Maghrebis) landed at Saint-Louis in Senegal. 'I am reinforcing them with twelve black cavalrymen,' the governor wrote to the French colonial minister a week later, and then proceeded to send his small cavalry on missions of 'pacification'. Their first feat of arms was to rout two thousand Tukulor warriors (a Muslim people from northern Senegal) on 4 August 1843.

As a result of this exploit, the colonial authorities decided to create a full squadron – and then a regiment – of exclusively Senegalese *spahis*, who went on to achieve glory in every corner of the French Empire. 'The sands of Mauritania, the banks of the Niger, the region of Timbuktu, the distant lands of Chad and Central Africa and … Morocco can bear witness to their heroic deeds,' proclaimed General Jung, commander of West African troops, in December 1927.

By the time Senegal gained independence in 1960, and after more than a century of loyal service, this prestigious cavalry regiment had almost been disbanded. However, the first president of the new Republic of Senegal, the poet Léopold Sédar Senghor, decided to retain a mounted squadron that would become part of the national police force. Despite Senegal's new-found republican status, the squadron's colonial past continued to be reflected in its spruce uniforms and its Barb horses, although these no longer came from Algeria but from Morocco, a country with much closer links to Senegal, both geographically and politically.

Resplendent in red tarbooshes, burnooses and jackets, and black baggy trousers, this parade unit is called the Red Guard. Today it is the only one of its kind in Africa, with the exception of the much smaller guard of honour created by the President of Togo, between 1975 and 1980, quite simply because he did not know what to do with the horses given to him by his northern neighbour, the President of Niger. Its only function is to parade through the streets of the capital once a year during the national festival.

42 • The twelve-year-old **Barb** stallion *El Ouassal* (by *Ouassal* out of *Assila*), owned by Madame Elgosi and presented by David Jollivet at the Haras du Pin Stud Farm (Normandy).

45 • *Naïm*, a fifteen-year-old **Barb** stallion, born in Algeria, owned by Eckehard Pöppel, from Süstedt (Germany).

46, 47 • *Guerrouan*, a palomino **Arab-Barb** (with light mane and tail) born in Morocco in 1995 and the pride of the stud farm owned by Susanne Geipert in Laubach, Germany. The crossing of Barb and Arab horses, especially in Morocco, created a type known as the Arab-Barb, which is finer than the pure-bred Barb.

49 • **Barb** and **Arab-Barbs**. Captain Djiby Tine holding *Tango*, from the band of the Red Guard, ridden by Warrant Officer Abdoulaye N'Diène and flanked by members of the 2nd troop.

51 • Mounted on **Barb** and **Arab-Barb** horses, the Senegalese Red Guard, photographed at their barracks in Dakar, in May 2003. *Saphir*, ridden by Sambou Diouf of the 1st troop of the Red Guard, is flanked by members of the 1st and 2nd mounted squadrons of the Senegalese national police force under the command of Captain Djiby Tine.

Barbs and Dongolas: trading places

Although separated by one of the largest deserts in the world, North Africa and Sub-Saharan Africa – the Maghreb (from the Arabic for 'west') and the Sudan (from the Arabic *bilad as-sudan* meaning 'land of the black peoples') – have maintained trading links for thousands of years. Twentieth-century French ethnologist Henri Lhote was able to prove this ancient link when he found evidence that the 'Sea Peoples' had travelled from Tripoli (the capital of present-day Libya) to Gao (in the east of Mali). Three to four thousand years ago, a 'chariot route' linking the shores of the Mediterranean and the banks of the Niger was already in existence. Far from being an insurmountable barrier, the Sahara has always been a region of trade and trafficking – some trades more honourable (salt) than others (slaves).

Of course, horses were also part of this vast trading network, which still continues today. The horse drinks large quantities of water and did not adapt well to the arid climate of the Sahara. Nor did it fare any better in the humid climate of the tropics, which favours the proliferation of the tsetse fly – a blood-sucker that transmits a deadly parasite causing 'sleeping sickness' in humans and a similar disease ('nagana') in domestic animals. It was a different story in the vast expanses of the Sahel, a broad belt of savannah between the desert and the tropical forest that roughly covers northern Senegal, the whole of Mali and Burkina Faso, the north of Togo, Benin, Nigeria and Cameroon, and the whole of Niger and Chad. Here, the horse adapted and even flourished, establishing a bloodline and developing numerous indigenous varieties that colonial vets attempted to describe, but which were mostly of Barb origin. They are smaller and a little narrower on the forehand than their North African ancestors, but they have nevertheless retained the general appearance that makes them easily identifiable.

The Dongola is another type of horse that is fairly widespread in Sub-Saharan Africa, recognized primarily by its strangely shaped head and very pronounced Roman nose. Its ancestry is obscure and unproven, although its champions maintain that it originated in Nubia and possibly even Yemen.

The horses of Sub-Saharan Africa (pages 53, 55, 57, 58, 59, 60 and 61) are descended from Barbs and Dongolas.

53 • *Ndjirou Balewou*, a six-year-old *fantasia* horse owned by the *lamido* ('lord') of Maroua and presented by Ibrahim, a dignitary from the lamidate of Mindif (Cameroon).

55 • *Balewou* (whose name means 'black'), a five-year-old from Bornu (Nigeria) presented by Souleyman, a 'warrior' from the lamidate of Mindif (Cameroon).

56 • His Majesty Oumarou Maigari, the lamido ('lord') of Mindif/Moulvoudaye (Cameroon), surrounded by his dignitaries.

57 • *Bidi Bridji*, a six-year-old *fantasia* horse – winner of the '1,500 metres' at the 'festival of the sheep' and of the race held on 11 February (the 'festival of youth') – presented by Abdulwahabou, a dignitary from the lamidate of Maroua (Cameroon).

58 • A three-year-old *fantasia* horse, whose name *Ndjirou Balewou* is in fact a reference to its colour – squirrel-grey, i.e. reddish grey. He is presented by Abdoul Karim, the dignitary responsible for the caparisons and other harness of the local *lamido*, and the official in charge of 'administrative affairs'.

59 • The five-year-old Pourou *Balewou Koppi* (whose name literally means 'flecked black-grey'), owned by the *lamido* of Mindif.

60 • *Bodewou* (i.e. 'red' or 'chestnut'), an eight-year-old ridden by Harun, the son of a dignitary from Maroua, an important lamidate in northern Cameroon.

61 • *Pourou* (which literally means 'tobacco flower', i.e. grey or blue-grey), a seven-year-old of unmistakable Barb origin, ridden by Abba, the son of the dignitary who is looking after the horse for the local lord, the *lamido* of Mindif.

The Musey: hidden strengths

Long before Africa's colonization, vast empires – often ruled by gallant black knights – had been established south of the Sahara. Among these was the Mali Empire, whose great ruler Mansa Musa (r. 1307–32) devalued his kingdom's gold reserves by liberally handing out the precious metal during his famous pilgrimage to Mecca in 1324. Then there was the Songhai Empire of Sonni 'Ali (r. *c.* 1464–92) and his successor Muhammad Askia, and the empire of Kanem-Bornu, on the shores of Lake Chad, whose horsemen, clad in their thick padding, resembled knights in a European jousting tournament.

In the early nineteenth century, the Fulani of Adamawa (a region situated in present-day Cameroon) created religious and military 'commanderies' by the juxtaposition of neighbouring states. With the advent of the Europeans at the turn of the nineteenth and twentieth centuries, these became known as 'lamidates', quite simply because the local overlords bore the title of *lamido* ('lord').

After colonization, these local 'sultans', as they were sometimes also known, retained their religious and social authority but lost much of their warrior status. However, their horses – and especially their stallions – remained the symbol of their power.

Today, horses are still the prerogative of chieftains and the *lamido* continues to entrust his horses to vassals known as *lawan* (chiefs of large villages), whose grand-sounding titles are now largely redundant and devoid of any real significance. These *lawan* are obliged to feed and care for the horses, and keep them at their lord's disposal – not, as in the past, for use in military campaigns, but for the festivals, ceremonies and *fantasias* that are reminiscent of former splendours.

These horses, the distant descendants of the horses that came from the Maghreb, Egypt and possibly the Arabian Peninsula, 'are of mixed character, somewhere between the Barb, Dongola and Arab', explains French researcher Christian Seignobos, who is a top specialist in the field.

Seignobos, who is also a geographer, ethnologist, linguist and zoologist, has a particular interest in a small member of the horse family. At 11.3–12.1 hh (119–124 cm), its origins are uncertain but it is 'trypanotolerant' (i.e. immune to the tsetse fly) and well adapted to swampland (see *Le poney du Logone*, 1987). It is still used today by the Musey, a non-Muslim people living on either side of the Chad-Cameroon border, on the flood plains of the River Logone. According to certain historians, this is where an ancestor of the great Russian poet Aleksandr Pushkin (1799–1837) was born in the late seventeenth century.

'Ridden bareback and in a makeshift bridle, Musey ponies were for a long time used for hunting and raiding,' says Christian Seignobos. 'The Musey invested them with human characteristics and their lives, like the lives of their human masters, followed a ritual pattern. When they died, they were buried and mourned.'

63, 65 • Two **Musey** ponies. On the right: *Gofna*, ridden by Marcus Jimanga. The photograph was taken beneath the sycamore figs near the concession of the chief of the province of Gobo (in northern Cameroon).

Jennets and Andalusians: in a league of their own

Never tell a *rejoneador* (mounted bullfighter) that his horse has North African blood in its veins. He is certain to deny it, even though certain historical events leave little room for doubt. In *c.* 200 BC, Numidian (and therefore Berber) horsemen crossed the Iberian Peninsula during the Carthaginian expedition against Rome. They were followed by Zenete (and therefore Berber) horsemen eight hundred years after the birth of Christ, and the Almoravid and then Almohad (and therefore Berber) dynasties, which ruled Andalusia for more than eight centuries and gave rise to one of the most brilliant civilizations in the Mediterranean world. Supporters of the breed are just as adamant: the Spanish horse is not related to the Berber horse, and the Iberian breeds have not been modified in any way since they were first introduced by the Iberians during the Neolithic Period. If you insist, however, some people will admit that perhaps there could have been some degree of foreign influence, but in the opposite direction. It was the invaders' horses that were improved by the native breeds.

To keep everyone happy, it was decided that the existing names and classifications had to be changed. In the 1960s, the extremely fashionable eighteenth-century term 'Spanish Jennet' was abolished, probably because it evoked the North African influence – according to linguists, the term 'Zenete' gave rise to *jinete* (the Spanish word for 'rider') and, consequently, 'jennet'. It was also decided to stop using 'Andalusian' since it could apply to a horse bred in Spain or Portugal. The two countries eventually established their own stud books and new names for their horses. When referring to Iberian breeds, it is now de rigueur to refer only to the PRE – Pura Raza Española (pure-bred Spanish horse) – and the PSL – Puro Sangue Lusitano (pure-bred Lusitano).

This all seems a bit clinical. Fortunately, however, a few enthusiasts continue to perpetuate the tradition (possibly inherited from the Berbers) of singing their horses' praises. Angel Peralta (b. 1926) – a famous Spanish breeder of bulls and horses, brilliant horsebreaker and remarkable horseman – does not let a day go by without composing a poem dedicated to the horse.

67, 69 • The **pure-bred Spanish** stallion *Tejedor VII* (by *Pegador* out of *Tejedora V*), ridden by Juan Antonio Martinez Ruzafa, technical director of the Peña de Bejar Stud Farm.

70–71 • The remarkable horseman and breeder Angel Peralta on his **pure-bred Spanish** horse *Capricio*, photographed in the Plaza de Toros de la Real Maestranza (Seville).

72 • The **pure-bred Spanish** horse *Cañamon*, presented in front of the monastery (La Cartuja) of Jerez de la Frontera by Antonio J. Diaz Porras, a former student of the Real Escuela Andaluza del Arte Ecuestre, in Jerez. The purest pure-bred Spanish horses are known as *cartujanos* (Carthusians) because they are descended from a line of magnificent horses bred by Carthusian monks in Seville (from 1393) and Jerez (from 1478).

73 • Three **pure-bred Spanish** brood mares from the Marques de Velilla Stud Farm, in San Pedro de Alcántara (near Malaga). The photograph was taken in Germany at 'Equitana 2003', a biennial equestrian event that shows breeds from all over the world.

The pure-bred Spanish horse: master of *haute école*

Whatever you call it – Iberian, Andalusian, Spanish Jennet or PRE (Pura Raza Española) – the Spanish horse is one of the jewels of the equine race. Enthusiastic testimonies to the qualities of the breed abound in the – often extremely literary – treatises on the art and practice of horse riding that proliferated from the sixteenth century onwards. In 1593, a certain Salomon de La Broue (1530–1610), equerry in the royal stables of the French King, Henri III (1551–89), wrote: 'I put the true Spanish horse in first place, giving it my vote as the most beautiful, the most noble, the most graceful, the most courageous and the most worthy of a King.'

Its conformation is so proportioned that it never fails to captivate even those who admit to knowing nothing about horses. Whether grey or black – all colours are accepted, except piebald and chestnut, according to the official standard for the PRE – it is certainly a magnificent animal. Yet there is also something very reassuring about it. It is not particularly large – 14.3–15.3 hh (150–160 cm) – and has a beautifully curved outline, from its aquiline nose, its powerful, arched neck, its broad back and its rounded hindquarters.

All these flowing curves undoubtedly help to create the impression of the placid and even temperament that people find so appealing. Those who have anything to do with the Spanish horse stress that this is not just a matter of appearances; these horses are incredibly kindly disposed towards their peers as well as their riders. Even the stallions (in Spain, the colts are not gelded) are docile, generous and cooperative.

This unique combination of physical attributes and 'moral' qualities has long been recognized by the masters of the world of equestrian arts. In France, François Robichon de la Guérinière (1688–1751) – riding master by royal appointment (1715) and director of the royal manège of the Tuileries (1730–51) – wrote (1731): 'All writers [on the subject] have given preference to the Spanish horse and regarded it as the best breed for schooling, because of its agility, its scope and a cadence naturally suited to pomp and ceremony, because of its proud bearing, gracefulness and nobility.'

The breed is so closely linked to the development of the equestrian art that it is tempting to ask which came first. Was it the use of this beautiful animal with its extraordinary natural abilities that gave rise to *haute école*? Or was it the Spanish horse that provided horsemen with the ideal tool and enabled them to develop and perfect their art? Today, the Spanish horse remains the preferred choice for *haute école* riding (with its 'airs above the ground') and equestrian displays.

75, 76, 77, 78, 79 • Two **pure-bred Spanish** horses, trained to perform by the famous stuntman and trainer Mario Luraschi - *Toreo* (aged eleven), performing 'circus tricks' (sitting down, bowing and rearing), and *Rimbaud* (aged nine), ridden by Joëlle Balland.

The pure-bred Lusitano: a star in the making

Another jewel of the Iberian Peninsula, the Portuguese horse or Lusitano is as deserving of praise as the Spanish horse. The horses are descended from the same Andalusian stock and have the same qualities, to the extent that, until recently, little distinction was made between these two branches of the same 'breed'.

The Portuguese branch became the Lusitano in 1966 and then the PSL or Puro Sangue Lusitano (pure-bred Lusitano) in 1990. Like its Spanish counterpart, it enjoyed its golden age with the development of the equestrian academies and *haute école*, a discipline in which it shows a particular aptitude. Between the sixteenth and eighteenth centuries, it was the darling of the royal courts of Europe.

In the nineteenth century, however, the crowned and titled heads of Europe suddenly became infatuated with Oriental (Arab, Turkoman and Persian) horses and their finest Western offshoot, the English Thoroughbred. They lost interest in academic equitation and the beautiful pirouettes and caprioles performed by the Iberian horses, and turned their attention to flat racing and steeplechasing – i.e. sport and the turf – or, to use the phrase coined by French author Jérôme Garcin in *Perspectives cavalières* (2003), 'horizontal' rather than 'vertical' equestrian disciplines.

This infatuation with Arabs and English Thoroughbreds all but sounded the death knell for the horses still classified as 'Jennets' and 'Andalusians'. It also threatened the future of the academic equitation they had helped to develop, a style of riding that the Portuguese horseman Diogo de Braganca called 'riding in the French style' (in 1975), even though it was first developed and subsequently revived in Portugal.

The first European treatise on the equestrian art was in fact written by an eminent Portuguese horseman – King Duarte of Portugal (1391-1438) – who, in around 1434, wrote a training treatise entitled *O Livro da ensynnança de bem cavalgar* toda sella ('A Book on How to Ride Well on All Types of Horse').

Five centuries later, after a long period of unpopularity and relative obscurity, the Iberian horse and the beautiful light, floating style that it executes so perfectly finally enjoyed a revival of interest. This was down to the brilliance of the Portuguese riding master Nuno Oliveira (1925–89), described as 'the most remarkable horseman of the twentieth century' by his disciple and friend Michel Henriquet, who has done so much to promote Oliveira's international reputation.

Used in Portugal for what are modestly referred to as bullfighting spectacles, the Lusitano is a true performer, well suited to the circus ring and footlights. Its colour is more varied than that of the Spanish horse and it often has a much fuller mane and tail, which merely adds to its charm, not to say its 'femininity'. Today the Lusitano is much sought-after by circuses, equestrian theatres, horse operas and equestrian 'academies' which, in the wake of Bartabas's carefully choreographed 'Zingaro' horse shows, are becoming increasingly popular throughout the world.

81 • The ten-year-old **Lusitano** *Jardineiro*, owned by the Rahmatallah family (England).

83 • The **pure-bred Lusitano** *Pintor*, ridden by Portuguese rider Rodrigo Brito de Moura Coutinho Torres, demonstrating a classic movement from Doma Vaquera – a form of riding inspired by the *vaqueros* (herdsmen) of southern Spain, open to all horses of Andalusian origin, i.e. Spanish horses and Lusitanos.

84, 85 • The twelve-year-old **pure-bred Lusitano** *Dao de Courenne*, from the Delgado Stud Farm (one of the best known in France), which also produced *Templado*, the world-famous star of equestrian theatre, magnificently trained and presented by Frédéric Pignon and Magali Delgado.

The Camargue: wild at heart

The Camargue, the vast marshy delta formed by the Rhône River as it flows into the Mediterranean, is famous for its *manades* – the Provençal term for the herds of wild horses that seem to thrive in the region's suffocating summer heat and bitter winter cold. Picking their way through the marshes, the occasional snowy-white egret perched on their backs, the Camargue, the small white ponies native to the region, seem locked in a time warp.

To its enthusiastic supporters, the Camargue pony is virtually identical to the horses that early man drove over a cliff to their death in their hundreds at Solutré in Macon – apparently so their flesh could be eaten, although this has not been proven conclusively. Standing between 13.1 and 14.1 hh (135–145 cm), sturdily built (300–400 kg/660–880 lb), robust and compact, the Camargue is also not totally dissimilar to the early prehistoric horses that were painted on cave walls, such as the Lascaux Caves in the Dordogne region of France.

However, it would be unrealistic to deny the possibility of any later influences, since there is evidence of Barb blood in the Camargue. This may have been introduced initially during the Roman period when Numidian horsemen, travelling from Carthage to Rome via Spain, must have passed through the region, but it was almost certainly injected later, during the Muslim conquest in the eighth century.

The question is purely academic. Whether they evolved in a vacuum, isolated from any form of external influence, or were crossed with some exotic breeds, today's Camargue ponies are unmistakable and well established as a type. They are also a protected species that is found nowhere else in the world – over three thousand wild horses living in an area of less than 100,000 hectares (247,000 acres) whose boundaries coincide roughly with those of the Camargue Nature Reserve.

Between May and October this 'Garden of Eden' can become a living hell, with horseflies, ticks, flies and mosquitoes. This does not seem to deter the thousands of tourists who make the annual pilgrimage to the land of *Crin Blanc* ('White Mane'), the cult film by Albert Lamorisse which, since winning an award at the 'Cannes Film Festival' in 1953, has captivated the hearts of millions of children worldwide.

Traditionally, all Camargue ponies bear the brand of their *manade* (herd) on their left hindquarter.

87 • The eight-year-old **Camargue** stallion *Gitan du Mas II*, presented by his owner Jean-Marie Nègre.

The Criollo: living the American dream

Paradoxically, the American continent, home of the 'Western' – where horses appear (at least in films) to be galloping off into the distance all day long, and where men seem to have been born in the saddle – was in fact the last continent to have been colonized by *Equus*, or the horse as we know it today.

According to the accepted history of the horse, millions of years ago, a small animal no bigger than a dog (30 cm/1 ft high), with four toes on its forefeet and three on its hind feet, was widespread throughout the continent of America. Known as *Eohippus*, it evolved gradually over the millennia, losing some of its toes as it developed into *Mesohippus*, *Parahippus*, *Merychippus* successively, finally disappearing from the American continent to pursue its evolution in Eurasia, where it assumed the 'definitive' appearance of the modern horse. It was not reintroduced into its distant land of origin until a few thousand years later – by the Conquistadors.

Palaeontologists were more or less unanimous on this point. At least until March 2003, when a research team in Peru discovered the complete skeleton of a horse, a 'proper' horse of the *Equus* type, that appeared to be three hundred thousand years old. If it were confirmed, this discovery would not only overturn the accepted theories on the subject, but also provide yet another example of the shaky foundations on which some of our knowledge is based.

Certain episodes in the history of the horse are rooted more firmly in legend than science, but there are a few incontrovertible historical facts. Having found America devoid of horses on his first expedition to the New World, when Christopher Columbus embarked on his second voyage he took some horses with him. He originally thought he had discovered India (which is why its inhabitants were originally known as Indians), but he had in fact landed on the Caribbean island of Hispaniola (now Haiti and the Dominican Republic). Although the exact number of horses he took with him on the caravels (the small, fast ships on which he made the voyage) is not known, it is thought to have been about twenty. It is recorded that Columbus landed on Hispaniola on 28 November 1493. The first horses to step onto the soil of the New World were with him.

Five years later, the island's horse population had evolved into a breeding stock comprising some sixty or so brood mares. Stallions were regularly brought in from Spain, and breeding was soon extended to the Caribbean islands of Cuba and Jamaica and the nearest regions of Central America. Even so, horses continued to be imported – into Panama in 1514, Mexico in 1519, Argentina in 1534 and Florida in 1538.

As top Argentinian horse expert Angel Cabrera explained in his book on American horses (*Caballos de America*, 1945), the breeding programme was extremely successful owing to the excellent climatic conditions and quality of the grazing in the newly conquered lands. It was also helped by the traditional Spanish practice of allowing mares and foals to run free, which meant that the horses that escaped or were simply abandoned eventually formed semi-wild herds that interbred. This was how an indigenous 'breed', a creole horse (i.e. born in the country), a truly American horse was created: the Criollo.

88–89 • A **Criollo** from the 'La Estrella' *cabaña* (cattle ranch) presented, somewhere on the Argentinian *pampas*, by José Ismael Britez.

91 • The seven-year-old **Argentine Criollo** *Miriju Noche Mala*, owned by Señor Duchini ('La Margarita', Ranchos, Argentina).

93, 94, 95 • The **Argentine Criollo** *Ayacucho Coscorron* with his trainer Martin Hardoy.

97 • José Ismael Britez, wearing spurs but no boots.

The Argentine Criollo, Polo pony and Petiso: born survivors

Aimé Tschiffely was instrumental in discovering and publicizing the qualities of the Argentine Criollo, helping it to become a kind of national symbol for the Argentine. A Swiss teacher, he was educated in England but lived in Argentina. He had been teaching in a secondary school in Buenos Aires for nine years when, in 1925, he decided to give up his job and travel. Tschiffely resolved that if he were going to travel he would do it properly. He decided to cross the Americas from south to north, from Buenos Aires to Washington DC. Originally he had intended to finish the journey in New York but decided to change his final destination after two fairly serious accidents.

To make the journey more interesting, the young Tschiffely (he was thirty-three years old) decided to avoid populated areas: 'Remote from cities and seaports – far from white men's haunts – ran much of my lonely trail. One night camp might be pitched far from any human habitation; again, I ate and slept with ancient Indian tribes in stone villages older than the Incas' (*Tschiffely's Ride*, 1933).

The only means of transport suited to such an undertaking was the horse. Many people thought he was quite mad to attempt such a thing, but Tschiffely proceeded with his plan and contacted a dedicated horse breeder. Dr Emilio Solanet applauded his project and recommended the virtues of the Criollo, explaining that they were 'the descendants of a few horses brought to Argentina in 1535 by Don Pedro Mendoza, the founder of the city of Buenos Aires. These animals were of the finest Spanish stock, at that time the best in Europe, with a large admixture of Arab and Barb blood in their veins.' Furthermore, Dr Solanet had just what Tschiffely needed – two Criollos, *Mancha* and *Gato*, sixteen and fifteen years old respectively, an advanced age for an ordinary European saddle horse but not for a Criollo.

Mancha and *Gato*, who stood about 14.3 hh (150 cm), had belonged to a Patagonian Indian chief named Liempichun ('I Have Feathers'). They had recently arrived in Buenos Aires with a batch of horses from Patagonia and were still half wild. A European horse lover would have found them curious to look at, to say the least. *Mancha* ('The Spotted One') was reddish-brown (chestnut) with large, irregular white markings (i.e. skewbald).

He had a white face and white stockings on each leg. *Gato* ('The Cat') was more or less the colour of milky coffee (dun), what Americans call '*buckskin*'. Tschiffely wrote: 'Their sturdy legs, short thick necks and Roman noses are as far removed from the points of a first-class English hunter as the North Pole from the South. "Handsome is as handsome does," however, and I am willing to state my opinion boldly that no other breed in the world has the capacity of the Creole for continuous hard work.'

It was on these fairly unprepossessing horses that the quiet and unassuming schoolmaster achieved one of the greatest equestrian exploits in history. He left Buenos Aires in 1925 and arrived in Washington DC three years later, completing a journey of 16,000 km (9,940 miles) that took him across frozen deserts and through tropical swampland, across the Andes and the Panama Canal, through half of Argentina, Bolivia, Peru, Colombia, the republics of Central America, Mexico and finally the United States. Incredible as it may seem, at the end of this amazing journey, Mancha and Gato were bursting with health.

Returning home (by boat), *Mancha*, *Gato* and Tschiffely were given a hero's welcome and a place in the history books. People who still harboured reservations about the Criollo, which they regarded as too rough and ready, common and coarse, suddenly discovered all kinds of qualities in the breed. It was used, most notably, to 'create' a new breed of horses that today dominates the world of polo – the famous Argentine Polo pony.

Obtained by crossing Thoroughbreds from North America (Anglo-Americans) and Criollo mares, and then re-crossing the results with Anglo-Americans, standing at 14.3 hh (150 cm), the Argentine Polo pony inherited the finesse and speed of the Thoroughbred, while retaining the stamina and resilience of the Criollo.

Another Argentine 'breed', the Petiso, is also the result of the skilful cross-breeding of European ponies and Criollos.

99 • The four-year-old **Argentine Criollo** *Bonito*, presented by Angel Gonzalez, his wife and their children.

100, 101 • The three-year-old **Argentine Polo pony** *Ombucito Impacto* (by *Infidente* out of *Loca*), presented (on the left) by Carlos Ulloa and (on the right) by Hilario Ulloa.

102, 103 • Two **Argentine Petiso ponies**. Left: The Petiso mare *Bragadense Celosa* (by *Labra Careta* out of *Bettina*), owned by Ernesto J. Figueras and presented by Daniel Meaca. Right: *Martin Fierro Mancho* (by *Charina Pacaflor* out of *Brava Lenteja*), owned by Anna Renata Hahn de Schultz and 'ridden' by her son Ferdinand.

Chile, Peru and Mexico: adding a touch of flamboyance

As additional proof of the Spanish and, even more distant, Berber influence on anything and everything related to horses in Latin America, much of the tack and equipment still used by modern *gauchos* and *vaqueros* (stirrups with a broad tread, bits fitted with curb chains and rowelled spurs) bears a striking resemblance to that found in North Africa. The Zenetes – one of the Berber tribes to go to Spain during the Muslim conquest – rode with short stirrups, a style of riding that became known as *a la jineta*. In his account of the conquest of Peru, in The Royal Commentaries of the Inca (1609), Garcilaso de la Vega ('El Inca'), the son of a royal Inca woman and a Spanish nobleman wrote that his land was conquered *a la jineta*.

'The modern Chilean Criollo originated in Peru, when it was still known as the viceroyalty of Castilla La Nueva (New Castile),' explains French enthusiast Gérard Barré, who has dedicated an entire website to the Criollo (www.justacriollo.com). 'The journey from Peru to the valleys of central Chile was so arduous that only the best and most robust horses reached their destination. These horses founded a line of Criollos that were among the most popular in South America. It was also one of the most isolated from outside influences due to the nature of the terrain, but also due to the wily local breeders who created a form of stud book in 1893, at a time when the concept of pure-bred horses was not particularly widespread in America'.

The Chilean Criollo has an aptitude for herding cattle and performs well as a rodeo horse. It also has great endurance, speed and beauty, with a thick mane and tail. Despite its relatively small stature (13.3 hh/140 cm), it has great capacity for hard work and is sure-footed with elegant paces.

It was these flamboyant, and sometimes highly elevated, paces that other Latin American countries tried to develop and accentuate in their own horses, not only for aesthetic reasons but also for increased rider comfort. By carefully selecting the horses most gifted at this type of dancing gait (*paso*) – which should not be confused with the traditional paces of 'ordinary' horses, the airs of *haute école* (e.g. *piaffe*, *passage*) or the extravagant movements (e.g. the *pas espagnol* or 'Spanish step') developed by European riders – they finally created such 'breeds' as the Paso Fino (Puerto Rico, Colombia), the Peruvian Paso (or Stepping Horse) and, more recently (1972), the Mexican Azteca.

105 • *Zafiro*, a young **Peruvian Paso** gelding (by *Galante* out of *Gloria*), presented by his owner Laurence Bouteiller from Arces-Dilo (France).

107, 108, 109 • The **Chilean Criollo** *Malulo*, presented and ridden by rodeo rider Marcello Rivas. *Malulo* belongs to Italo Zunino, the owner of the fundo San Lorenzo, at the foot of the Andes, in the Bío-Bío region of Chile.

Native American horses: the mysterious Appaloosa

In Native American culture, there are all kinds of charming legends to explain the first appearance of the horse in America. According to a Kiowa legend, for example, this extraordinary animal was born of the dream of an old medicine man, while the Apache and Blackfeet peoples attribute its paternity to the sun and water – or rather the spirit of the sun and the spirit of water. A Hopi legend tells the story rather differently: 'On the day that humans emerged from the bowels of the Earth, the Great Spirit, in the form of a bird, gave each one a language and a race'. The white men, 'always impatient', began to walk towards the south. When they were exhausted, 'a woman tore off pieces of her skin and fashioned them into horses'.

The interesting thing about this legend, apart from the fact that it attributes the origin of the horse to a woman, is that it identifies the white man as the first to own this legendary creature.

Italian-born researcher Maria Franchini has gathered together many different stories recounting the first encounters of many Native Americans with the white man and therefore their very first contact with the horse (*Les Indiens d'Amérique et le cheval*, 2001). A Comanche tale is particularly vivid – 'One day, the Comanche, at the time when they travelled on foot with their dogs, noticed some strange animals in the distance. They were almost as big as a buffalo and had long necks and a hump on their back that reflected the light of the sun.' The large humps in question were of course the Conquistadors clad in armour. The strange animals approached and one of them suddenly began to make sounds. 'As it began to speak, the animal split in two. The large hump that reflected the light detached itself from the animal's body and took a human form. The other part now looked like a large dog…

The story continues in this vein for several hours and ends, after a great many twists and turns, with the following episode: 'One night, as the "humps-that-reflect-the-light" were sleeping, the Comanche stole their large dogs… The Comanche learned to ride these animals and became one of the most powerful tribes of horsemen in the West. As for the white men, they learned to walk.'

The reaction of the native peoples on their first contact with horses was not always as humorous. Most accounts of the conquest of the New World indicate that, for the most part, the South American Indians were terrified when they came across these huge, unfamiliar animals.

The incident most often recounted tells how a single Spanish horseman succeeded in routing the entire Inca army without doing a thing – he simply appeared in front of them on his horse. This happened in Peru, in 1534, more than forty years after the first European horses had arrived in America.

However, as the conquering forces and settlers advanced, penetrating further inland, sometimes preceded by whole herds of runaway horses that had returned to the wild, the Indians became accustomed to them and soon learned how to use these large animals to their own advantage.

The peoples of North America did not discover the horse until much later, but it only took another fifty years for the use of the horse to spread to the Plains Indians, and by 1650 the Apache had become formidable horsemen. They were followed by the Comanche, Navajo and Shoshone who, during their extensive travels, passed on this new 'weapon' in their armoury to the Cayuse. The latter must have proved particularly skilled at breeding horses as, by the nineteenth century, all Native American ponies were known as 'Cayuse ponies'.

The Cayuse Indian pony proper is relatively small – about 13.1 hh (135 cm) – and can be any colour. It has a full mane and tail, and a heavy head that is almost too large for its body, but it has an intelligent eye and, above all, amazing stamina and endurance. According to the journal (1867) of Colonel Philippe Régis Denis de Keredern de Trobriand – a French aristocrat and volunteer general in the Army of the Potomac, who came to the United States in 1841 – 'the Indian pony can cover distances of 110–130 km (70–80 miles), from dawn to dusk, without stopping, while most of our horses are exhausted after 55–65 km (35–40 miles)' (Franchini, op. cit.).

For a long time it was believed that Native American ponies were all descended from the escaped horses that the Spanish referred to as *mesteño* ('wild' or 'untamed'), a word that mutated into the term 'mustang'. However, this theory is contested today since it has been proven that the Native Americans acquired most of their horses fully broken, either by trading or quite simply by stealing entire herds.

As for the Cayuse Indian pony, one school of thought is that it was the result of haphazard cross-breeding between horses from South and North America – Spanish horses with Barb blood and French carriage horses brought to Canada by the early settlers.

The only thing known for certain is that, in the past, the Native Americans – like the Americans and an increasing number of Europeans today – were very keen on what are known as pinto (painted) horses in the United States and coloured horses in Europe, i.e. piebalds, skewbalds and horses with spotted, speckled, marbled or flecked markings.

One of the most sought-after types of marking is the 'leopard' pattern, one of the six characteristic patterns of the Appaloosa horse, attributed to the Nez Percé Native Americans whose territory was crossed by the River Palouse (hence *Palousa* and Appaloosa). Since 1938, when The Appaloosa Horse Club was first established, the Appaloosa has been regarded as a 'breed' in its own right in the United States, and more recently in certain European countries – even though its distinctive markings have existed in a number of other breeds for centuries, such as in Mongolia, Russia and Denmark. Several works of art bear this out, such as *The Piebald Horse* (Getty Museum, Los Angeles) – an Appaloosa – by Paulus Potter (1625–54), the Dutch artist famous for his paintings of animals, and the lithograph produced by Jean-Baptiste Oudry (1686–1755) to illustrate the chapter on horses in the comprehensive *Histoire naturelle* by the French naturalist Georges-Louis Leclerc de Buffon (1707–88).

113 • The ten-year-old **'English' Appaloosa** *Spottie Dot Com*, ridden by Sophie Broome, daughter of the owner and niece of the famous showjumper David Broome.

114 • Two **'German' Appaloosas**, *Coco* (aged eight) and El *Lobo* (aged seven), owned by Herbert Fischer and presented by Paul Herrada.

115 • The three-year-old **'Canadian' Appaloosa** mare *Wyalta Kamia*, presented by her owners Donna and Syd Wyatt.

The Mustang: symbol of a nation

The horse is now an integral part of American legend and the history of the United States. When some of the most momentous events in American history are called to mind, they bring with them a rush of evocative images – a miner galloping into town to have a nugget of gold weighed, horses pulling a string of covered wagons as settlers make their way west, a line of Native American warriors atop a ridge surveying the distance while their horses fidget and shuffle beneath them. So many of the American heroes – from General Custer (1839–76) and Chief Crazy Horse (c. 1842–77) to Buffalo Bill (1846–1917) and John Wayne (1907–79) – were intrepid horsemen. When John W. Russell created the Pony Express weekly mail service in April 1860, he made it possible to send a letter across the United States, from Washington DC to San Francisco, a distance of 3,000 km (1,875 miles) in just ten days, thanks to a relay system that leaves you breathless just thinking about it. Horses were changed every 20 km (12 miles) and riders every 120–160 km (75–100 miles).

Many Americans have a great deal of affection for the horse, which has become a spirited symbol of freedom and wide, open country and a form of national mascot, second only to the bald eagle. It is also true to say that, of all the horses in America, the people have a particular soft spot for the Mustang. No ordinary horse, the Mustang really is a 'breed' apart – a distant descendant of the 'large dogs' brought over from Spain by the Conquistadors in the late fifteenth century. The first Native Americans to see the horse believed it to be some form of supernatural being. Subsequently, having escaped from – or been abandoned by – their Spanish masters, these horses returned to the wild where they were subjected to the harsh process of natural selection. As a result, they developed an extremely strong constitution and an extraordinary vitality, spreading 'like wildfire' throughout the American continent, especially in North America.

'Wild' is not quite the correct term since only animals that have never been tamed by man can be truly classified as 'wild'. Domestic animals that have returned to the wild are usually described as 'feral', although 'wild' is a stronger term with more exciting and even glamorous connotations. It is certainly more in line with the image that rodeo enthusiasts like to project of the proud and impetuous, 'untameable' 'bucking broncos'. This only makes the deft skill and great speed with which the Native Americans were able to tame and ride these 'wild' horses all the more remarkable. It also makes the methods used by the modern 'horse whisperers' – popularized by Nicholas Evans in *The Horse Whisperer* (1996) – all the more admirable. The methods used to win the confidence and 'break' or 'start' these horses are described in detail by Monty Roberts in *The Man who Listens to Horses* (1996).

Today, American Mustangs are becoming increasingly less 'wild'. In the early twentieth century there were almost two million Mustangs, so many that they were becoming a nuisance and were even regarded as 'vermin' since they damaged crops and monopolized grazing. Like their Australian counterparts, the Brumbies, they were hunted relentlessly and almost wiped out. There are currently only a few thousand of these horses left, carefully contained and controlled on vast reservations.

Still, the Mustang has managed to survive its fall from grace and has emerged from its

long ordeal with increased stature and an air almost of martyrdom. Today, redefined as part of the national heritage, it is a protected species and the object of much care and attention on the part of the many enthusiasts belonging to numerous conservation associations. Some, like the Spanish Barb Breeders Association (SBBA), stress the Mustang's Barb and Spanish origins. Others, who want to immortalize it as the horse of the Blackfeet, have formed the Blackfeet Buffalo Horse Coalition (BBHC).

116, 117 • American Quarter Horses undergo rigorous training. Deep in the Rocky Mountains, on pastures grazed by his hornless Black Angus cows, William Kriegel breeds around fifty **Quarter Horses** per year. As well as his Montana ranch, Kriegel also owns the famous La Cense Stud Farm (near Rambouillet, in France). In the space of a few years, La Cense has become the Mecca of what some people refer to as 'natural horsemanship' and is where one of the best-known American 'horse whisperers', Pat Parelli, teaches his famous 'method'.

119 • *Digger*, a **Mustang** owned by Jessica Russell.

121 • Robert Black Bull – founder of the Blackfeet Buffalo Horse Coalition, on the Blackfeet Indian Reservation, Browning (Montana) – presents one of his favourite **Mustangs**. Robert Black Bull is fighting to have these horses reintroduced into the wild and, among other things, has devised a youth empowerment programme to encourage young Native Americans to become involved in the protection of the breed.

122 • *Dolly*, a **Mustang** presented by the Russell family. From left to right: Cody, Lisa, Bob, Jessica and their dog Grace.

123 • *Strip*, a **Quarter Horse**, presented by the Griffith family. From left to right: Bob, Wyatt (aged six), Bud, ranch foreman, his wife Cheryl and Hallie (aged eight).

The Quarter Horse and Morgan: true success stories

As a horse-loving nation, the United States has produced some truly remarkable breeds. The oldest, best known and most widespread of these breeds is the American Quarter Horse, which numbers almost four million worldwide. Its unusual name derives from the fact that it was bred, in the early seventeenth century, by the English settlers of Virginia and Carolina (on the East Coast) to take part in races run over a quarter of a mile (about 400 m). This relatively short distance required horses that could make lightning starts with a great capacity for acceleration.

The Quarter Horse, probably a cross between horses of Spanish and English descent, gradually became the prototype of the cowboy horse, the ideal all-purpose horse that was both lively and intelligent. It is what its many supporters call a 'complete horse', with a fine, muscular neck well set on powerful, sloping shoulders, a broad, deep chest, a short, muscular back, strong loins, massive, rounded hindquarters, clean, hard legs, and a character that is obedient and eager to work, with good 'cattle sense' (i.e. well suited to driving and 'cutting' cattle). Robust, fast, courageous and reliable, this medium-sized horse (14.3 hh/150 cm) is one of the great success stories of American breeding.

The other great success is the Morgan which, although less well known outside the United States, is just as interesting. The origins of the breed were purely fortuitous. It began in the late eighteenth century, in a small town in Vermont, in the north-east of the United States. The town's singing master, a good man named Justin Morgan, had lent some money to a friend who, unable to repay him, settled his debt with a horse. The horse – a young stallion named *Figure*, born in the neighbouring state of Massachusetts – was of doubtful origin, although its sire may have been a Barb and its dam a Welsh mare. It was small (14 hh/142 cm) and compact, with a kind temperament. Not knowing what to do with it, Morgan rented it out as a stud horse. Amazingly, all its offspring proved to be stocky and courageous bays (with a black mane and tail) – just like their sire.

When the horse's owner died, it was on loan to Robert Evans, a local farmer, who put it to work in the fields, whilst at the same time continuing to use it at stud. The valiant little horse continued to produce identical foals, strong and generous, regardless of the mare. It finally came to the attention of the army and was bought and used as a 'professional' stallion on one of the army stud farms. Renamed *Justin Morgan* in honour of the late choirmaster, this exceptional horse died in 1821 at the advanced age of 32, leaving a line of robust and versatile horses that were in constant demand for the US cavalry until the army became mechanized.

The many exploits performed by these versatile horses – which worked equally well under saddle, in harness, or as draught and packhorses – feature prominently in the golden legends of the Wild West. One of these is the story of *Comanche*, the only horse to survive the famous Battle of Little Bighorn (25 January 1876). In spite of its many wounds, it lived for many years and regularly took part, saddled and bridled but unmounted (a sign of mourning), in many commemorative ceremonies.

Slightly smaller and stockier than the Quarter Horse, the Morgan founded several other typically American breeds: the Missouri Fox Trotter, the Tennessee Walking Horse and, more recently (nineteenth century), the

American saddle horse. Today, these breeds are primarily selected for their exaggeratedly high action in paces such as the 'fox trot', 'running walk', 'flat foot', 'slow gait' and 'rack', which are extremely popular in the United States. Although they present quite a spectacle, these gaits are not always natural and sometimes involve practices (the use of artificial aids, surgical intervention, etc.) that are not permitted in Europe.

125 • *Montana's GC Tracer*, a **Missouri Fox Trotter** owned by Neil O'Peterson and presented by Tymbre.

127 • The cowboys of La Cense Montana ranch: Bud Griffith, Bob Russell, Dan Hill, Dick Chaffin and Bob Griffith, and their **Quarter Horses**.

The Orient: improving Western breeds

If there is a Garden of Eden for the horse, then it must be in the sumptuous lands of the Orient, lying somewhere between the Red Sea and the Bay of Bengal. It is a region that encompasses three worlds, civilizations and languages: Persian, Turkic and Arabic. This is the origin of the supreme horse breed, the star of the equine world and the stud horse that improved the horses of the West: the pure-bred Arab. Whether it is entirely pure or not, or even entirely Arab or not, its blood flows in the veins of most European breeds – racehorses and sporting horses, saddle and draught horses, leisure and warhorses, all have shared this common ancestry.

The Arab truly is one of the most beautiful horses on Earth, and many people are extremely passionate about this amazing creature. Even those who are not particularly interested in horses are struck by its grace, elegance and flamboyance. Spirited and noble, it has a fine head, with large, expressive eyes, dished face and flaring nostrils, and a good coat, high tail carriage and light, airy movements. Its fiery temperament adds a hint of danger.

Thousands of suras, verses, proverbs and legends sing its praises and acclaim its qualities. The Arab people in particular believed that this horse embodied the qualities of all other breeds. In *The Horses of the Sahara* (*Les chevaux du Sahara*, 1853), General Eugène Daumas, French consul at Mascara and an expert on Barbs, Arabs and the traditions of North Africa, said that it has the courage of the wild boar, the grace of the gazelle, the light-heartedness of the antelope and the speed of the ostrich.

The fertile imagination and poetic genius of the Arabian storytellers really came into their own when they recounted the origins of the horse and how one of the most arid regions in the world (Arabia) could have become the birthplace of one of the most beautiful 'breeds' of horses in the world. They say that it was all quite simple, although there are several versions of the same story. The best known is related in a Bedouin legend: 'Then Allah took a handful of the South Wind and he breathed thereon, creating the horse and saying: "Thy name shall be Arabian, and virtue bound into the hair of thy forelock…. I have preferred thee above all beasts of burden….'

However, some people prefer a more scientific explanation of the Arab's origins, choosing to stick to the theory that this horse adapted gradually from horses imported two or three centuries before the advent of Islam, from Mesopotamia, Turkey, Iran and even Central Asia, by the Bedouin of the Nejd region. This is the only region on the Arabian Peninsula that provides grass for grazing, thanks to the streams of water running down from the high plateaux.

Ultimately, it does not really matter. Arguments between the experts concerning the real or supposed origins of the Arab horse have become irrelevant at a time when the breed is scattered all over the world, and its finest examples no longer come from its land of origin. Today, the breed includes horses of very different types and sizes – between 13.3 and 15.3 hh (140–160 cm) – depending on where they are bred, the preferences of their breeders and the uses for which they are intended. This is in spite of the best efforts of a centralized organization – the World Arabian Horse Organization (WAHO) – which, since it alone is qualified to decide whether a horse is a pure-bred Arab or not, has acquired an omnipotent status.

During the latter half of the twentieth century, it was the Americans who became the world's principal breeders of Arab horses. Today, over half of the 500,000 officially registered pure-bred Arabs are to be found in the United States, where they are all too often selected on purely aesthetic criteria and paraded solely in shows that are little more than glorified beauty contests – the equine equivalent of 'Miss World'. Some truly beautiful horses have been bred in order to compete in these contests, but they are often maladjusted temperamentally and quite useless as saddle horses. Indeed, the practice seems ill-advised for an animal that owes much of its reputation to its riders' martial exploits.

In Russia, Arabs tend to be bred for their speed. One of the world's largest stud farms for pure-bred Arabs is the Tersk Stud near Pyatigorsk, on the foothills of the Caucasus Mountains. Meanwhile, the Arab countries are trying to reconcile the requirements for both physical beauty and nobleness of temperament. They continue to produce animals that are both beautiful and loyal, spirited and robust.

Some fine examples of pure-bred Arabs from the stud farm of Sheikh Hamad bin Khalifa al-Thani, Emir of Qatar. Situated about 15 km (9 miles) from the capital Ad Dawhah (Doha), the stud was established in the early 1990s, near Ar Rayyan, the scene of a historic Qatari victory over the Turks at the end of the Ottoman Empire.

128 • *Roba Al Shaqab* (by *Safir* out of *Rabaab Al Shaqab*), a pure-bred **Arab** born in 2003, held by Jassim Al Kabi.

132, 133 • *Adnan Al Shaqab* (by *Al Adeed Al Shaqab*), a pure-bred **Arab** born in 2001 and champion colt of Qatar in 2002.

134, 135 • Three pure-bred **Arab** yearling fillies (by *Gazal*) from the Al Shaqab Stud Farm: *Roba Al Shaqab* (centre right), *Enshoda Al Shaqab* and *Al Noof*.

136–137 • *Al Adeed Al Shaqab* (centre), an eight-year-old pure-bred **Arab** of Egyptian descent and world champion in Paris in 2002, presented by Ahmed Mousadaq at Umm Said, near Ad Dawhah (Doha). On the left, the mare *Imperial Jaliisah* is ridden by Ali Ismael Al Bakir.

The pure-bred Arab: really pure, really Arab?

One more bone of contention between the English and French is the matter of who was the first to introduce the Oriental horse to the West. Apparently oblivious to the fact that both nations could have discovered it during the Crusades, each continues to claim the merit for this discovery.

The British assert that it was King James I (1566–1625), son of Mary Queen of Scots and a keen horse-racing enthusiast, who first had the idea of importing Oriental stallions to cover English mares, with a view to increasing the strength and stamina of local horses and improving their performance.

The French maintain it was Napoleon Bonaparte (1769–1821), who was extremely impressed by the small horses ridden by the Mamelukes (a warrior caste) during his famous Egypt expedition (1798–99). It has been said that, while he may not have succeeded in overwhelming Egypt entirely, he was certainly inspired by the quality of the horses he found there and lost no time in adopting them for his own use.

Some of these horses have earned a place in history. *Ali* (or *Aly*), a 14.2 hh (147 cm) grey stallion (the Arabs never geld their horses), was brought back to Europe and ridden by Napoleon (as First Consul) at the Battle of *Marengo* (1800) and (as Emperor) at the battles of Essling and Wagram (1809). Another was Marengo (who is often confused with *Ali*), a smaller (13.3 hh or 140 cm) iron-grey stallion captured at Abukir (1799). He accompanied Napoleon throughout his career until the Battle of Waterloo (1815) where he was wounded, captured and taken back to England. He died in England in 1832, at the age of 38, and his skeleton can still be seen today in the National Army Museum in London.

However, the comprehensive inventory of the Emperor's horses, drawn up by Philippe Osché in *Les Chevaux de Napoléon* (2002), reveals a disturbing fact: most of the horses referred to as 'Arabs' probably did not belong to the Arab breed as it is known today. At the time, there was little regard for the niceties of modern ethnology. 'Arab' was a generic term and was used indiscriminately to refer to all Oriental horses. Arabs, Barbs, Terskys and Turkomans (Turkmens), as well as Ottoman, Kurdish, Persian and even Ethiopian horses were all grouped together under 'Arab'.

The same principle was applied to the groups of ethnic people: the famous Mamelukes encountered by Napoleon in Egypt did not have much in the way of Arab blood in their veins. This warrior caste was composed of former slaves from Central Asia, the Caucasus and even the Balkans.

Some fifty years later, the situation had changed very little. In 1862, General Daumas was still able to write: 'Call him Arabian, Barb, Turk, Persian, Nedji, it matters little for all these terms are but baptismal names. The name of the family is the Horse of the Orient' (*The Horses of the Sahara*). It also fuels the arguments of those who are now challenging the Arab origins of the 'Arab' horse and assert that Europeans did more than discover it – they created it!

This opinion is obviously not shared by the Arab nations. Since the 1970s, they have made every effort to re-establish links with their glorious equestrian past by creating specialist stud farms in Morocco, Jordan, Saudi Arabia and the Gulf States – today regarded as among the best in the world – and by reviving practices traditionally associated with the horse, such as falconry.

The horses in the photographs on pages 139 to 145 are all pure-bred Arabs.

139 • *Safi Al Shaqab* (by *Safir* out of *Poema*), born in 1997 and champion stallion of Qatar in 2001, ridden by Ahmed Mousadaq, at Al Hamla.

141 • A Qatari falconer. Hunting is one of the favourite pastimes of the Arab people of the Gulf states.

142 • *Al Adeed Al Shaqab* with the Al Qadi family.

143 • *Wazmeia* (by *Al Adeed* out of *Dalilat Albadeia*), held by Mahmoud Abdelfatah Badair.

144 • *Al Adeed Al Shaqab*.

145 • *Aliah Al Shaqab* and her filly foal.

Fortunately, there are a great many people who want to prevent the pure-bred Arab from being cast in the role of simply improving other breeds and/or being used purely as a show animal. To this end, they continue to promote its qualities of endurance and speed in an increasing number of specialist events. For example, one of the most recent 'World Endurance Championships' was held in Dubai, in 1998 – when Sheikh Mohammed bin Rashid al-Maktoum himself took part – and races reserved for 'small' horses are regularly run in France (Cagnes-sur-Mer), Russia (Pyatigorsk) and the Lebanon (Beirut). The following two photographs were taken at the Hippodrome du Parc, in Beirut.

146 • The six-year-old pure-bred **Arab** *Rayan* ('radiant'), owned by Henri Chalhoub and presented by jockey Joseph.

147 • The four-year-old pure-bred **Arab** mare *Faten* ('beautiful'), owned by Nabil de Freige and Moufid Dabaghi, and ridden by jockey Farouk.

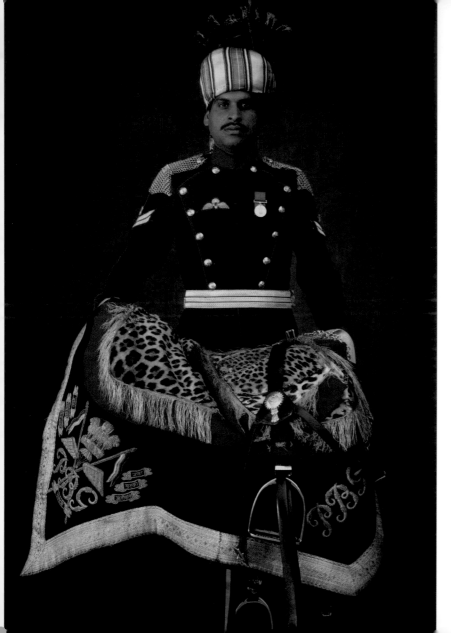

150, 151 • A prestige regiment, the Indian Presidential Body Guard is mounted on dark-bay, almost black, horses. Only the trumpet major has a grey horse. On the ceremonial saddle, covered with leopardskin, the initials PBG (Presidential Body Guard) are embroidered in gold.

The English Thoroughbred: the fastest horse in the world

'The horse is not one of man's conquests – even the most beautiful – but rather one of his *products* (possibly the most beautiful)... the result of human genius, the pure product of culture.' This is how artist Christian Renonciat describes the horse. As a sculptor, he gives pride of place to horses in his work. The English Thoroughbred is a pure creation – a pure product, to use Renonciat's term – one of man's finest 'inventions' and one of the great success stories in the history of man's domestication of the horse. The result of the work of several talented breeders, it is quite simply a work of art, a masterpiece.

There is no real standard against which to measure the Thoroughbred, and it can stand between 15.1 and 17.3 hh (155–180 cm). English anatomist, painter and engraver George Stubbs (1724–1806) skilfully depicts it in his paintings, however. He excelled at painting these large and elegant but spirited creatures, at a time when the breed was becoming established and already beginning to dominate the racecourses.

What follows is not a detailed description of the breed's complicated ancestry, with its multiple lines of descent, but rather an outline of its origins. James I, originally James VI of Scotland until, in 1603, he was crowned James I, King of England, Ireland and Scotland – was the founder of the Newmarket and Epsom races. He is thought to have been the first person to have had the idea of improving the progeny of English mares by putting them to Oriental stallions. His grandson Charles II (1630–85) wanted to perpetuate the tradition and complete what his grandfather had started, but on a much grander scale. He sent trusted envoys to the Levant and Maghreb to bring back a number of fine stallions. The royal envoys scrupulously fulfilled their mission and returned home with the breeding stock – Turkoman, Barb and Arab mares and stallions – that formed one of the cornerstones of the breeding programme, which would soon produce a new strain of racehorse. These animals were tried and tested on the racecourse, selected for their speed and improved with new injections of 'Arab' or comparable blood.

According to the record books, three stallions used to improve this new breed came to be regarded as the foundation stallions of the Thoroughbred dynasty: the Byerley Turk, a bay brought to Yorkshire *c.* 1690, the Darley Arabian, a dark bay imported from Aleppo (Syria) in 1704, and the Godolphin Barb or Arabian, another dark bay whose story deserves special mention.

Born in 1724, the Godolphin Barb was one of a number of horses given to Louis XV of France (1710–74) in 1731 by the Bey of Tunis. The horse was not to the French King's taste and he ordered it to be removed from the royal stables. It was duly sold and ended up in harness on the streets of Paris. An Englishman travelling through the city bought it and took it back to England where he sold it to a publican, who was a racing fanatic. Having raced the poor creature somewhat unsuccessfully, the publican sold it on, this time to Lord Godolphin, a former royal treasurer, Member of Parliament and enthusiastic horse breeder, whose successes were more a matter of luck than judgment. He did not immediately recognize the qualities of his Barb, which was relegated to the role of 'teaser' until it managed an unplanned covering of a beautiful chestnut mare named *Roxane* and proved itself to be a good sire. The stallion had finally found its rightful 'niche' and has been known as the Godolphin Barb ever since.

The Godolphin Barb's line of descent includes *Matchem* (b. 1748), a horse that was also descended, via its dam, from the Byerley Turk. The latter's line of descent includes Herod (b. 1758), also descended from the Darley Arabian via his dam. In the Darley Arabian's line of descent, *Eclipse* (b. 1764) was descended – via his dam – from the Godolphin Barb. *Matchem*, *Herod* and *Eclipse* were the first generation of the great Thoroughbred dynasties. The descendants of the best known, *Eclipse* (so called because he was born during an eclipse of the sun), have included more than a hundred winners of the Epsom Derby, Britain's foremost flat race. In *c.* 1770, George Stubbs painted a portrait of this exceptional horse – an extremely rangy animal, with an arrow-like head, long neck, slender body and long, fine, powerful legs, that was evidently built for speed. It was the prototype for what from then on came to be known as the English Thoroughbred. It should be pointed out, however, that 'English' describes the origin of the breeders rather than the horses, while the term 'Thoroughbred' denotes an exceptional animal, but one which is the result of quite a mixture of breeds.

Today, the Thoroughbred has become an international breed and there is therefore a tendency to drop the adjective that alludes to the 'Englishness' of its origins and simply refer to it as the 'Thoroughbred', a much more appropriate term that reflects the purity of its breeding. This is how the Americans, who have become its principal breeders, tend to refer to it. Whilst England continues to be a major centre for the production of racehorses, it only ranks third in terms of the number of foals dropped each year – approximately ten thousand, compared with twenty thousand in Australia and almost fifty thousand in the United States. A number of other countries also produce Thoroughbreds: France, Germany, Italy and, above all, Ireland, which also has some of the finest stud farms for the breed, along with those of Kentucky in the United States.

This internationalization is due to the fact that horse racing, which was born in England, has now spread throughout the world. The races offering the most prize money are run in Japan and Dubai, but Hong Kong, Moscow and New Delhi also have major racetracks, and the stakes are also high in the African capitals of Dakar, Cotonou and Ouagadougou.

With such big prize money now at stake, stud fees have soared. At the last estimate, a single service by the stallion *Stormcat*, owned by a famous stud farm in Kentucky, cost half a million dollars, while a yearling filly – which, to use racing jargon, could turn out to be a 'champion' or a 'dead loss' – was knocked down for two million Euros at a recent auction (August 2002) in Deauville (France), one of the centres of the international Thoroughbred trade.

This beautiful filly, whose name was *Vimy Ridge*, was bought by Sheikh Maktoum Al Maktoum who, with his brothers, is currently one of the top racehorse owners in the world, with over six thousand horses scattered between a dozen magnificent stud farms in Europe, the United States and his own country, the United Arab Emirates.

The families that currently dominate the world of racing hail from Europe (the Wildensteins), America and Japan, but the most influential come from the East, such as the famous Ismaili dynasty of the Aga

Khans. By investing their fortunes in the development and improvement of the English Thoroughbred, the Orient has once again come to the aid of the West.

The horses in the photographs on pages 152–153, 154, 155, 159, 161, 162–163 and 164 are all English Thoroughbreds.

152–153 • The Gilltown Stud in County Kildare, Ireland, has three first-class stallions – *Daylami*, *Sinndar* and *Kalanisi* – which, put to carefully chosen brood mares (e.g. the three-year-old mare *Banadiyka*, presented here under a sycamore by Joe Dempsey), produce the superstars of the future.

154, 155 • *Daylami*, a grey stallion born in 1994 (by *Doyoun* out of *Daltawa*), the first champion in the world to win seven Group 1 races. On the right, *Daylami* is presented by his handler Liam Foley.

159 • *Sinndar*, a bay stallion born in 1997 (by *Grand Lodge* out of *Sinntara*), the only horse to have won the Derby, the Irish Derby and the Prix de l'Arc de Triomphe in the same year.

As well as being great horse-racing enthusiasts, the English have another great passion – fox-hunting – and have created a horse specially for that purpose, although it is also extremely well suited to other equestrian sports such as showjumping and eventing. The Hunter is the result of crossing Thoroughbreds with hardy horses.

161 • *Ivanhoe*, a seven-year-old **Hunter** owned by Mr Adsetts (Badminton) and presented, in the style of a painting by George Stubbs, by Matthew Laurence (complete with top hat).

162–163 • At a flat-out gallop on the Curragh racetrack, south of Dublin, in Ireland. *Morning*, a four-year-old grey mare (by Ali Royal), owned by Stephen Hayden and ridden by Lesley MacCormack, and High Living, a three-year-old bay filly (by Diesis), owned by Lady O'Reilly, ridden by Nicola Shadwick and trained by John Hayden (Stephen's father).

French saddle horses: rooted in history

Before any major construction work can be undertaken in France, regulations stipulate that the soil and substratum of the site must be carefully examined. This typically French invention, known as preventive archaeology, is regarded as a pointless and pernickety precaution that has greatly irritated developers, public works contractors and highways engineers by curtailing their activities. However, just a few years ago, the policy proved to be completely vindicated.

In November 2001, before work could begin on the new bypass planned for the town of Clermont-Ferrand, capital of the Auvergne region, excavations were carried out on the site, in accordance with regulations. On this occasion the archaeologists made an amazing discovery. They uncovered a tomb containing eight men, lying one behind the other, the left arm of each resting on the shoulder of the man in front, and eight horses, carefully laid on their right side, their heads pointing to the south. Although the exact causes of their death and the circumstances and meaning of this Gallic burial are unknown, it does reveal a great deal about the very special relationship that has always linked horse and man in this ancient land.

Before France was sanctified following the conversion of the Frankish king Clovis I (c. 466–511) in AD 500, it was known as Gaul. It was named after the beloved daughter of Epona (meaning 'Divine Horse'), the Gallic horse goddess whose cult was adopted by the Roman cavalry.

For centuries, Gaul had been a sort of vast experimental breeding ground that gave rise to many different types of horses. A rich land at the crossroads of Europe, it was also a place where many different cultures became intermingled. Continually subjected to a wide range of influences, it frequently fell victim to the avaricious nature of the peoples who came on horseback to occupy or just pass through from all four corners of the Earth – Celts, Huns, Goths, Franks, Vandals and Moors. They came from the east and the north – from the Steppes of Asia and the depths of the Germanic lands – and from the south – from the Iberian Peninsula and even from as far afield as North Africa. It was these invasions – whether their effect was civilizing or destructive, whether they were Berber or Barbarian – that helped to make France the land of four hundred horses. Paradoxically, this early chaos also gave rise to a culture of order and of the methodical turn of mind and love of logic that became the dominant characteristic of French civilization.

It would be impossible to explore all the twists and turns of the horse's amazingly rich history in France. Therefore, it seems appropriate to turn directly to the story behind the creation of the French saddle horse. After World War II, it was decided to rationalize the breeding of an animal that mechanization had rendered useless, or of much less use, by merging the many different types of saddle horses that had been so carefully and patiently adapted for various purposes in each region. In 1958, it was ruled therefore that there would be no more Norman or Anglo-Norman (also known as half-bred) horses, no more local breeds like the Vendéen, Charollais, Angevin or Bourguignon. Instead, there would be just a single 'breed' known as the French saddle horse.

Thanks to its many different origins, fifty years after this enforced integration, there are still many different types of French saddle horse. One of these, defined somewhat negatively as the AQPS – Autre Que Pur Sang (which translates as 'other than Thoroughbred') – is bred exclusively for racing. However, it is mainly in the field of events such as dressage, showjumping, cross country and eventing that the 'breed' tends to excel today, with such examples as *Galoubet* (descended from a line founded by English Thoroughbreds) and *Jappeloup* (descended from a line of trotters) which, ridden by Pierre Durand, won a gold medal at the Seoul Olympics in 1988.

The other major 'breed' of 'French' saddle horse is the Anglo-Arab. It was created in the nineteenth century by Eugène Gayot (1808–91), one of the most eminent French hippologists of his day and a veterinary surgeon (like his father, who was for a time inspector of the Neapolitan stud farms of Joachim Murat, one of Napoleon's most celebrated marshals and King of Naples). In 1840, Gayot became director of the Haras du Pin Stud Farm, where he promoted the introduction of English Thoroughbred blood into the local breeds, thereby producing the Anglo-Norman which was unfortunately lost a century later in the great melting pot of the French saddle horse. When he became director of the Haras de Pompadour, in 1843, he had the opportunity to realize a long-standing dream – to combine the speed of the English Thoroughbred with the endurance of the Arab.

The result was a big thoroughbred horse (over 16.1 hh/165 cm) that was elegant but powerful, a very distinguished horse with outstanding paces and 'bags of personality'. While it can sometimes be difficult, the Anglo-Arab can also put its heart and soul into the task in hand. Used in AQPS races, dressage and showjumping, it is above all in cross-country events that its qualities shine through.

In France, four 'Thoroughbred' breeds are recognized and promoted by the national stud farms: the pure-bred Arab, the English Thoroughbred, the Anglo-Arab and the French saddle horse.

164, 165 • The sixteen-year-old **English Thoroughbred** and former champion racehorse *Al Capone*, by *Italic* (by *Carnaval* out of *Bagheira II*) out of *L'Oranaise* (by *S'Agaro* out of *Paris jour*), presented on the right by Dominique Bœuf and Olivier Peslie, and accompanied on the left by the students of the École des Courses Hippiques (Gouvieux, France).

169 • The **Anglo-Arab** stallion *Quain* (by *Emir IV* out of *Maïa du Vent*), bred at the Haras du Pin Stud Farm, in Normandy.

171 • The **English Thoroughbred** stallion *Freedom Cry* (by *Soviet Star* out of *Falling Star*), placed second in the Grand Prix de Paris in 1995. One of the top stallions at the Haras du Pin Stud Farm.

172, 173 • The **French saddle** horse. Left: The four-year-old *Lou du Veret*, presented by his owner Agnès Juhel-Anfray. Right: Two brood mares 'with foal at foot', presented by their owner Arsène Aubry.

174, 175 • The nine-year-old **French saddle horse** stallion *Hors la loi II*, by *Papillon rouge* out of *Ariane du Plessis II* (by *Joyau d'Or*), ridden by the famous Brazilian champion Rodrigo Pessoa at the Haras de Ligny Stud Farm (Belgium).

176, 177 • *Koala d'Ivraie*, a five-year-old **Anglo-Arab** stallion (by *Belo des Vernières* out of *Aurore du Maury*), ridden by Gilles Marnay in the school at the Haras du Pin Stud Farm in Normandy.

178, 179 • The nine-year-old **French saddle** horse *Hortus de Pierre* (by *Papillon Rouge* out of *Sika du Rouet*), owned by the Haras du Pin Stud Farm (Normandy).

Trotters: France and further afield

Trot racing is a true passion in France. While breeding gallopers tends to be more of an aristocratic pursuit and remains the preserve of a relatively small number of wealthy horse lovers, trotters are often bred by country dwellers and farmers who own two or three brood mares and who breed, break in, train and race their horses themselves. 'There are about 7,000 people who dream of producing a champion, although they are reluctant ever to admit it' wrote an expert in the field, journalist Jean-Pierre Reynaldo in his book *Trotteur, quand tu nous tiens*, (roughly translated as 'The Passion Inspired by Trotters').

Very much a spectator sport, like football or cycling, French trotting attracts vast crowds and receives considerable media coverage. Trotting stars sometimes become national heroes, their fame reaching far beyond their already wide circle of fans. You do not have to be a cycling buff to have heard of Lance Armstrong and Bernard Hinault, or a soccer fan to recognize Beckham and Zidane. Similarly, if you live in France, you do not have to read the French racing newspaper *Paris-Turf* every day to be familiar with such evocative names as *Gelinotte*, *Roquépine*, *Bellino*, *Idéal du Gazeau*, *Lutin d'Isigny* and *Potin d'Amour*, or to have followed *Ourasi*'s glittering career. This French champion won the prestigious Prix d'Amérique trotting race three years in a row (1986, 1987 and 1988), before he was forced to surrender first place to a mare called *Queila Gédé* in 1989. He streaked to victory again in 1990, winning the race for a record fourth time – a first in the history of this world-famous event.

Ourasi's extraordinary career ended with this record and included fifty-eight wins, earning his owners over three million Euros (about two million pounds sterling), a world record for winnings by a trotter. It is no wonder that this kind of money inspires the dreams of ordinary people, particularly as Jean-Pierre Reynaldo rightly pointed out, 'There's no mystery to breeding trotters: good breeding stock produces good horses, but champions are often produced by sires that are not in quite such demand'. In other words, anyone could strike it lucky. As a result, around ten thousand foals are dropped every year in France.

Most of these horses will never see a racecourse in their life because they are only allowed to race after competing in speed trials. In order to qualify for a race they need to perform well in preliminary rounds and prove, for example, that they can trot 1 km (just over half a mile) in less than a minute and a half. As a comparison, Ourasi's personal best was 1 minute, 11.5 seconds over a distance of 1.6 km (1 mile) – equivalent to an average speed of 50.27 km/h or 31.24 mph.

What becomes of the thousands of horses that fail to make the grade? This is a taboo subject in the trotting world where those who are generally open and up-front can be rather guarded with or suspicious of outsiders. Although no one is keen to admit it, the truth is that horses that perform below par end up being sent to the slaughterhouse.

Fortunately, a lucky few do escape this fate – they are sold off cheaply and then retrained for equestrian tourism, hunting, riding, even endurance competitions in which they perform remarkably well. As a result of their rural origins, these fine horses can still travel long distances, although they are not always capable of racing at high speeds.

Usually good-natured, generous, energetic, sturdily built and fairly tall (between 14.3 and 16.3 hh/150–170 cm), French trotters can be used both under saddle and in harness although, strangely enough, this twofold ability is rarely exploited in racing.

Other countries, apart from France, organize harness races: the United States, which succeeded in developing an extremely swift trotter, the American Standardbred; Russia, the birthplace of the Orlov trotter, regarded as the progenitor or, at any rate, the benchmark for trotters throughout the world; and lastly Sweden and Italy, where this speciality breed is also well loved. However, France is virtually the only country where horses can compete in trotting races with jockeys. This form of racing is sometimes criticized for being somewhat farcical. Admittedly, it does lack the stylishness of harness racing, but a visit to the Vincennes racecourse, the world arena for trot racing, soon sets the record straight. Evening race meetings are particularly thrilling. You cannot fail to be gripped by the excitement of the event and the spectacle of such magnificent animals thundering down the course, pulling the sulky (light two-wheeled carriage) and its gaudily dressed driver behind them, wheels screeching on the black cinder track. For the trotting enthusiast, there are few finer sights.

Established in the mid-nineteenth century, the French trotter is a skilful mix of bloodlines: Anglo–Norman, English Coach Horse (Norfolk trotter), Russian trotter and English Thoroughbred. This breed is now challenging the American trotter for world supremacy.

183 • *Insert Gédé*, a six-year-old **French trotter**, owned by Joël Séché, trained by Jean-Luc Bigeon and presented by his stable lad Cyril Buhigné.

184–185 • *Kahela de Luc*, a five-year-old **French trotter** mare (by *Boss du Buisson* out of *Saldone*), winner at Vincennes and Enghien at the age of two, driven by Sylvain Devulder on the racetrack of the Grosbois Training Centre (Paris region).

Cob and Friesian: dual-purpose horses

Although the phrase has passed out of current usage to a certain extent, these horses used to be described as 'dual-purpose' because they could be either ridden or driven in harness. Not fast enough to be included in the saddle-horse category and not heavy enough to be regarded as proper draught horses, they were more likely to be harnessed to light four-wheeled conveyances, or together in teams of two, four or six to pull a stagecoach or carriage. The larger of these horses came to be known as coach horses. This general category of horses was once very widespread, but only a couple of breeds exist today.

Norman Cobs are still bred, albeit in small numbers, in the Saint-Lô region of France. They stand 15.3–16.3 hh (160–170 cm), but often weigh a hefty 700–800 kg (1550–1750 lb). Breeders use the evocative phrase 'close to the ground' to describe this horse, which has a somewhat angular conformation. Although stocky, it differs from 'heavy' horses because of its fine musculature, hard legs and elegant gait. This breed has both heart and stamina, which makes it a joy to ride and recalls its Anglo-Norman origins.

The origins of the Friesian breed are more difficult to determine. This horse is now extensively bred far from its birthplace of Friesland (in the Netherlands). As is often the case with horses, it is the successful product of a cross-breeding programme that seems to owe more to luck than to judgment. Not surprisingly, the Dutch are keen to trace its origins back to distant indigenous ancestors. However, this horse has clearly been crossed with Oriental stallions in the past and, although it is impossible to say by how much the breed was improved with any real accuracy, it is certain that it contains Barb, Andalusian and Arab blood.

This magnificent horse has great class with an all-black coat, proud carriage, a thick, flowing mane and feathers partly covering its hooves. It can obviously be ridden, but its beauty, grace and nobility are best observed when it is in harness, which is when it shows the true extent of its generous spirit, energy and enthusiasm.

It is easy to see how this breed has become such a firm favourite, even with people who have little or nothing to do with riding or driving horses. If French children want to adorn their bedroom walls with a poster of a horse, many will choose that of *Zingaro*, the wonderful Friesian horse owned and ridden by the renowned trainer Bartabas, who named his famous equestrian theatre after him.

Many people mourned when this magnificent animal died in 1998 on a tour of the United States. Obituaries were published in all the main newspapers, and even poets joined the ranks of the mourners: 'You, emblem of arrogance/you, roguish colossus who play/the mythological beast/and relish making time stand still/as the world fetes you like an idol,' wrote André Velter (in his book *Zingaro suite équestre*, 1998). 'You, whose galloping hooves pound the stones/you know that your might impresses/with its silver glints/but you have a tender gaze beneath your forelock/and faith, almost, in the mornings of the world.'

In equestrian terminology, the same words do not always refer to the same concepts all over the world. The word 'pony' is one such term, widely used in the US and UK to refer to any horse below a specific height (see page 268), while in France for example, it tends to refer only to specific breeds. The word 'cob' is another, referring in English-speaking countries to a general body type for horses (small and stout) rather than to a breed (as in French).

187 • *Denzil*, a four-year-old **Cob**, owned by Jill Day de Kinnersley and presented by Emma Bryan (Wembley, Horse of the Year Show).

189 • *Loukoum de Vallière*, a four-year-old **Norman Cob**, presented by his breeder, Norbert Coulon, with friends Aurélien Decaen, Jean Quiédeville, Pierre Bihel, Maurice Agnes and Christophe Colard, all breeders themselves.

190 • *Koert*, an eleven-year-old **Friesian** owned by Philippe Harcourt and presented by Ann Zagradsky.

191 • Trainer Fritz Deutschenbaut presents his **Friesians**: *Oege*, *Jakob*, *Douwe* and *Marcel*.

German horses: great sporting breeds

In his most famous novel *The Ogre* (*Le Roi des aulnes*), which won the 1970 Prix Goncourt (the top French literary award), Michel Tournier (b. 1924), a philosopher and scholar, describes 'an enormous black gelding, rippling with muscles and with rump and hair as ample as a woman's', on which the hero of the story, Abel Tiffauges, takes riding lessons. One day, his teacher, an old riding master called Pressmar, decides to tell him 'the truth' about the horse: 'Compare the dynamics of the horse with that of the deer, for example. All the deer's strength is in his shoulders and neck. But all the horse's strength is in his crupper. A horse's shoulders are fine and flat, just as a deer's crupper is thin and tapering. A horse's weapon is his kick, which comes from the crupper; a deer's is his antlers, the force of which comes from the neck. A deer moves by a sort of front-wheel drive; a horse impels himself forward by the motion of his hind-quarters. In fact, a horse is a crupper with organs attached in front.'

This particular description of the horse, which has since become an anthology piece in French literary collections, is also a good description of Tiffauges's mount, a Trakehner.

In the novel set in 1940 in East Prussia, the horse came from Trakehnen, a stud farm founded two centuries earlier by King Friedrich Wilhelm I (1688–1740) and enlarged by his son Friedrich II (1712–86), better known as Frederick the Great.

Five years after the episode related in Tournier's novel, the Soviets seized control of East Prussia. Fleeing the advance of the Red Army, officials in charge of the royal stud farm managed to take away with them a large number of brood mares during the harsh 1944–45 winter. However, the Russians did not lose all the Trakehners. They managed to salvage some mares and stallions and continued breeding for themselves, developing the breed in various stud farms scattered about their vast territory. In fact, in 1970 when Elena Petushkova became the world dressage champion and Olympic gold medallist, she was riding *Pepel*, a Trakehner as black as the coal mined in the Urals.

The original stud farm no longer exists, and the Trakehner is now bred in many places. This, coupled with the fact that over the past century it has occasionally been necessary to rebuild the breed by injecting large doses of

new blood (particularly English and Arab), has led the Germans to regard the Trakehner as an international breed – like the English Thoroughbred, the pure-bred Arab and the trotter (mainly of American origin), breeds that are all widely produced in Germany.

However, the German breeders owe their sterling reputation less to these 'federal' breeds and more to the diversity and quality of their 'regional' breeds. Unlike the well-intentioned French, who, just after World War II, combined local types of horse in a single major breed (French saddle horse), the Germans promoted the development of breeds peculiar to each of the *Länder* in the federal republic. This breeding policy has produced some remarkable results. In half a century, Germany has become one of the foremost producers of top sporting horses in the world and the leading producer in Europe.

A brief overview of the breeds, moving north to south, includes Holstein, Mecklenburg, Oldenburg, Hanoverian, Westphalian, Rhineland Heavy Draught, Hessian, Württemberg and Bavarian Warmblood. The Hanoverian, for example, is the result of judicious cross-breeding (Holstein + English Thoroughbred

+ Trakehner, in particular) and a rigorous, persistent process of selection. Standing at 16.1–17.1 hh (165–175 cm), the Hanoverian is a powerful jumper (cf. *Deister* who, ridden by Paul Schockemöhle, was voted 'Horse of the Century') as well as a first-class dressage horse. Not too highly strung, the breed is elegant rather than dazzling, reflecting contemporary requirements.

The Holstein, on the other hand, is a sturdy breed from north-west Germany and was an acclaimed 'dual-purpose' horse for many years before becoming the excellent sporting horse it is today. The breed was then lightened by the addition of foreign blood (once again English Thoroughbred) to meet new market demands. *Corlandus*, who was ridden in dressage by the French-German rider Margit Otto-Crépin, is one of the more famous examples of this breed.

195 • The **Russian Trakehner**, *Khan Baty*, a seven-year-old stallion, bred in the Tver region and presented by his owner Anatoly Inozemtsev.

196 • The **Hanoverian**, *Wolke VII*, a four-year-old mare, owned by Diedrich Meyer and presented by Anett Kumpe.

197 • Although the **Rhineland Heavy Draught**, *Valido's Boy*, is fourteen years old, he still has plenty of life.

198 • The **Holstein**, *Loutano*, a fifteen-year-old stallion, presented by Gilles Marnay at the Haras du Pin Stud Farm in France, but owned by the Holstein breeders' association in the Netherlands.

199 • The **Mecklenburg**, *Greif*, a four-year-old stallion, presented by Christian Heineking, an employee at the state stud of Redefin (Germany).

Italy: the art of horse riding

Horse lovers owe a deep debt of gratitude to Italy. However, it is too often forgotten that this country has given Europe several magnificent breeds of horses, as well as the first riding manual.

The first book on horsemanship to appear in a European language was written in 1245 by Giordano Ruffo, the Calabrian stable master at the court of Frederick II (1194–1250), Holy Roman Emperor, King of Germany and King of Sicily. Although this was not a proper manual of horsemanship (it was nearly two centuries before the Portuguese King, Dom Duarte, published a work worthy of this name, in 1434), it was an authentic veterinary treatise, which – according to French scholar Mennessier de la Lance – tackled 'breeding, foaling, schooling, bitting, shoeing, outward appearance and ailments with remedies for each one' (in his *Essai de bibliographie hippique*, 1915–21).

It was in the sixteenth century that Italy laid down the foundations of horse riding, later known as 'French equitation' because it flourished in France under the reign of Louis XIV. Nevertheless, the origins of horse riding can be traced back to Naples, Rome and Ferrara, where academies dedicated to the study of the equestrian arts proliferated during the Renaissance. One of the most famous of these institutions was Federico Grisone's academy, which taught dressage movements such as *piaffe*, *passage* and most of the 'airs above the ground' that form what is now known as *haute école*: *courbette*, *croupade*, *ballotade*, *pesade* and *capriole*.

Grisone's treatise *Gli ordini di cavalcare*, published in 1550, was translated into French in 1559. It also appears to have been translated into English, or at least adapted and abridged, by riding master Thomas Blundeville in 1560 as *The Arte of Ryding and Breakinge Greate Horses*. In Blundeville's book, he set out some excellent principles that still apply to riders today. For example, he said that it was vital to maintain gentle but firm pressure on the mouth to ensure that the horse was well-behaved and light on its feet. However, he also suggested some retaliatory measures to deal with stubborn horses that would now result in the intervention of the animal protection agencies. Some punishments were quite ordinary (shouting insults and hitting the animal with a stick) while others were much more inventive, entailing the use of burning straw, a cat tied by its back to a long pole and shaken under the horse's belly, or sharp spikes (sometimes a hedgehog) placed under the tail. Although such drastic measures may be shocking today, they were fairly standard practice at the time.

Cesare Fiaschi, founder of a rival academy to Grisone's in Ferrara, held slightly different views to those advanced by the Neapolitan master. He thought unresponsive horses should be treated 'harshly and roughly', but over-enthusiastic horses should be ridden 'in a friendly, gentle manner'. This was definitely a step in the right direction.

Things improved even further with Giambattista Pignatelli. A student of Fiaschi's, who was to become a famous riding master himself, he commented that riders should be 'sparing with their blows and lavish with their caresses', according to the French riding instructor Antoine de Pluvinel (1555–1620). After becoming the riding master of the (future) King Louis XIII (1601–43), Pluvinel wrote a treatise called *L'Instruction du roy en l'exercice de monter à cheval*, which is regarded as one of the seminal books of the renowned

French school of equitation and which, particularly after François de La Guérinière (1688–1751), acquired international acclaim.

Three centuries after giving rise to the *haute école* style of riding, the Italians continued their pioneering work, revolutionizing the equestrian world. It is probably not an exaggeration to say that one Italian, Federico Caprilli (1868–1907), invented competitive riding as it is practised today. He was the first to come up with the idea of jumping an obstacle not with the shoulders inclined backwards, one hand on the pommel and the other in the air, but, on the contrary, with shortened stirrups, leaning forwards over the neck. This is such a natural position that it is hard to see why it was not adopted until the early twentieth century.

Italy has also produced some exceptional horses. The Neapolitan tops the list and merits a short description, even though the breed became extinct long ago. Giuseppe Maresca, a dedicated breeder, is hoping to be able to rebuild it. This remarkable horse traces its origins back to the famous episode in Hannibal's Italian campaign that has become known as the 'Delights of Capua' (216–215

BC). The Carthaginian leader was keen to make a stop in this picturesque town in Campania (just north of Naples), as his army needed to rest before attacking Rome, and he wanted to enjoy the many pleasures on offer; he also sought fresh horses for his cavalry. Even then, Capua was famous for its horses, which were of Etruscan origin. These horses were probably crossed with the Punic horses (in other words, Barbs) that had been imported by the Carthaginians. Whatever the case, when Charles of Anjou (1285–1325) seized Naples almost fifteen centuries later at the instigation of the Pope and became King Charles I, he was staggered by the great Oriental beauty of the horses he found there.

The Angevin kings were replaced by the Aragon rulers, who succeeded to the throne of Naples in the fifteenth century. The Iberian horses they brought with them were crossed with local horses to produce the Neapolitan breed. Salomon de la Broue who, like Pluvinel, came to Naples to learn the 'new' art of equitation, wrote that the city produced horses that were perfect in beauty and gentleness.

This superb breed has not become completely extinct; it continues to live on through the Lipizzaner, the star of the famous Spanish Riding School in Vienna. With a special talent for performing pirouettes and other acrobatic movements required by the Austrian riding masters, the Lipizzaner are all descended from six stallions, two of which – *Neapolitano* and *Conversano* – were Neapolitans.

Twentieth-century Italy has remained a great equestrian nation with many breeds of racing, sporting and draught horses. Breeds of leisure horse include the Salerno, the Maremmana, a hardy saddle horse native to Tuscany with a great deal of stamina, and the Murgese, a vigorous, sturdy and good-tempered saddle horse native to Puglia.

203 • *Nottingham*, an eight-year-old **Murgese** stallion, owned by the forest rangers and presented by his rider Giuseppe d'Onghia.

204 • *U Rondinella*, a fourteen-year-old **Maremmana** mare, presented by her owner Stefano Meattini.

205 • *Zorro*, a thirteen-year-old **Maremmana** stallion, presented by his owner Miriano Manciati.

206, 207 • The nineteen-year-old **Lipizzaner** stallion, *Siglavy Alba* 56 (by *Siglavy III* out of *Alba 31*), owned by Maryse Flauder, from Gazeran.

Great horses: treasures of the past

If the great 'heavy horses' were man-made monuments of bricks and mortar, they would be towering cathedrals or impregnable fortresses. Over the centuries they have been bred and cross-bred to meet our various needs – war, farming, transport, industry – but have now ceased to be as useful as they once were. Does this mean that they should be condemned to disappear? Are they now in danger of fading into neglect like the monuments of the past? If so, we should do everything in our power to save them as they are as much a part of our heritage as our great buildings.

'To get on your high horse' is an expression commonly used to refer to someone behaving in an arrogant or superior manner, but its origins are in fact military. In the Middle Ages, no one could go to war without a 'great horse'. These massive horses were capable of carrying the enormous weight of the caparisons as well as the rider, who was also heavily armour-clad – a combined load in excess of 100 kg (220 lb). In order to avoid exhausting the horses before they were taken into battle, their heavy breastplates were only fitted at the last moment and they were not mounted until it was time to fight. These chargers were called destriers because they were led to the battlefield unsaddled and unmounted, their reins held on the right (or dexter) side of the knight or squire. The noblemen who rode horses were called chevaliers or cavaliers after the French word for horse (cheval), while the young men of gentle birth who attended on the knights and carried their shields (often decorated with their coats of arms or escutcheons) were called esquires.

For centuries, man has fashioned the horse according to his needs, enhancing qualities and developing breeds for specific purposes. The commonly held belief is that, after thousands of years regarding the horse simply as a source of food, man finally decided to domesticate it in order to take advantage of its speed as a mount. However, archaeological research reveals that domestication may have resulted from man's realization of the horse's strength. The earliest known evidence of man's use of the horse indicates that these magnificent animals were used in harness before they were ever ridden: 'The earliest cart with four wheels known to have existed was in Ur, in 3500 BC,' writes French anthropologist Jean-Pierre Digard (in *Le Cheval, force de l'homme*, 1994 and 2002), 'and although it was probably devised for oxen, it may then have been adapted for dziggetais (Mongolian wild asses) and donkeys by the Sumerians.' And subsequently for horses, enabling them to begin a successful career as draught animals, employment which only began to founder with the fairly recent advent of mechanization.

Although the first known horse-drawn vehicles originated in the Orient (the Hittites, Egyptians, Aryans and 'Sea Peoples'), it was in the West that the most effort was made to transform and 'improve' horses. The general idea was to make them broader and bigger, increasing their body weight without sapping their strength so that they could pull increasingly heavy loads. This tentative research, which involved continual cross-breeding and zoological experimentation, bore fruit during the mid-nineteenth century, at a time when agricultural, industrial and transport revolutions were radically changing the face of Europe.

The term 'heavy breeds' is indicative of this change in approach. There was once such a wide variety of great horses that they could be classified by speciality. Horses small enough to be ridden were called army horses. Horses bred to be equipped with a packsaddle were called packhorses, while those destined to pull light carriages were called coach, carriage or shaft horses (because they were harnessed between two shafts). A distinction was made between heavy and light draught horses. As one type of horsepower took over from the other with the appearance of motorized vehicles, these terms started to become less precise. People began to refer loosely to 'work' horses, 'utilitarian' horses, 'farm' horses, 'rustic' horses and, finally, 'heavy' horses.

Immediately after the invention of the internal combustion engine, men turned their backs ungratefully on their former constant companions, and horses were considered fit only for slaughter. Fortunately, many horse lovers are now trying to find alternative methods of employing them that will ensure their protection. Organizations such as Traits de Génie, a French association dedicated to the promotion and protection of draught horses, are to be congratulated for their fine work. The ILPH (International League for the

Protection of Horses) is the welfare branch of the FEI (International Equestrian Federation) and also does much to further the cause.

208 • This horse of rustic origins (probably **Comtois**) is now a stylish entertainer. Nine-year-old *Felous* has been taught *haute-école* airs by his owner Arnaud Gilette, proving that a 'heavy' horse can be nimble on his feet!

212, 213 • Two fine **Shire** specimens. Left: *Regius Victorious* (by *Black den Mascot* out of *Regius Jet*) presented by Stuart Harrison. Right: *Stanley House Duchess* and her foal *Stanley House John Bukk,* presented by Mrs Anne Hull.

215 • *Richard*, a **Suffolk Punch**, in full harness, presented by his owner Mrs C. J. Clark.

The Shire and Suffolk Punch: English gentle giants

The tallest horse in the world can stand 19.3 hh (2 m) high and weigh over a ton. The record is held by a nineteenth-century Shire stallion, *Samson*, which stood at an astonishing 21.2 hh (219 cm). The English Shire horse is not only the tallest, broadest and strongest heavy horse in the world, but it is also one of the oldest. Julius Caesar referred to a great black horse (*equus magnus*) found in the north of England, which was probably a distant ancestor of the Shire. Between the two breeds are centuries of hard work, breeding and cross-breeding with horses from northern Europe, particularly Flanders.

If the Shire's distant ancestor was as ugly, lazy and bad-tempered as has been documented, this is simply one more reason to praise the skill of the breeders who succeeded in producing an elegant horse (apparently by adding some Arab blood) that is so placid that it can be safely ridden by a child.

When people picture these gentle giants, many see them harnessed to huge brewers' drays, transporting heavy barrels from the breweries to the inns, a job they are rarely given now, except for publicity campaigns. After virtual extinction during the 1950s owing to the knock-on effect of widespread rural mechanization, over the past few years the Shire has regained numerous admirers and has even acquired new employers. It is estimated that there are now around three thousand Shire horses in existence. In 1981, *Farmer's Weekly* reported that a single breeder in the north of England had sold two hundred Shires in the past year to work in the agricultural or industrial sectors. The article was called 'Shires Help to Cut the Costs'.

England can still also boast the magnificent Suffolk Punch, another possible descendant of the famous *equus magnus* mentioned by Caesar. Native to the south-east of England, this compact breed (the nickname 'Punch' means short and thick-set) has a massive head, thick neck, muscular shoulders and short, powerful legs. It has clearly been bred for hard work. As with so many other horse breeds, there is a certain amount of debate surrounding its origins: the foundation stallion may have been *Blake's Farmer*, born in 1760, or a trotter eight years its junior, belonging to a Suffolk breeder, one Thomas Crisp from Ufford. However, it must have taken a great deal of cross-breeding to produce the present-day conformation and qualities of this breed. The first imported crosses probably date back to the thirteenth century and may even include descendants of Norman mares from the time of William the Conqueror (*c.* 1028–87).

The Suffolk Punch is a powerful, energetic and courageous horse. Put to work from the age of two, it is able to provide good and loyal service for at least twenty years on only a moderate amount of food. Capable of pulling heavy loads or ploughing for several hours without food or drink, it is the most frugal of the heavy horses. Nothing seems to shake its courage, spirit or gentleness. Its relatively small size – usually 15.3–16.3 hh (160–170 cm) – also makes it very manoeuvrable when working in urban areas. Farmers, on the other hand, value the lack of feathering on its legs, which makes these horses well suited to the clay soil of eastern England. In contrast, the legs of their English and Scottish relatives – the Shire and Clydesdale breeds respectively – are almost entirely covered in feathers.

217 • *Max*, a **Clydesdale** belonging to Linda Mac Ivor (Royal Show, England).

218, 219 • A Lance Corporal drummer, mounted on a **Clydesdale** called *Belisarius*.

German heavy horses: dependable characters

The commonest heavy horse in Germany comes from the Rhineland region. The result of cross-breeding not only between Rhineland breeds but also with those of Westphalia and Saxony, the line was strengthened in the nineteenth century by the introduction of the French Ardennais and Norman Cob (developed from half-bred horses) and most notably the Belgian Brabant (or Belgian Heavy Draught). It was not until the beginning of the twentieth century that the breed was considered fixed and was finally granted its own breed status, the *Rheinisches Deutsches Kaltblut* or Rhenish Westphalian Draught horse.

This is an extremely hardy horse, a dependable worker, quiet and manageable, with a compact and dense conformation, standing 15.3–16.1 hh (160–165 cm), with a thick neck, broad chest and short, muscular limbs. Since the Rhenish Westphalian Draught horse reaches maturity relatively quickly and only begins to show its age quite late in life, it is likely to give its fortunate owner long and faithful service. It comes as no surprise to learn that it has become Germany's principal draught horse, except perhaps in the southern region of Bavaria where it now has competition from a medium-weight draught horse – the Pinzgauer Noriker – that has adapted perfectly to the mountainous terrain. This horse is descended from one of the five bloodlines of the draught horse known as the Noric or Noriker (or South German Coldblood), which is believed to be the oldest in Europe.

Two thousand years ago, the Romans introduced the ancestors of this medium-sized horse (15–16.1 hh or 153–165 cm) into the Roman province of Noricum, which covered roughly the same area as present-day Austria. They developed the strong, gentle, even-tempered and, more importantly, sure-footed horse, which they needed for agricultural and forestry work, as well as for transport in mountainous regions.

In the sixteenth century the introduction of Andalusian and Neapolitan blood into the stock gave the Noriker character and agility. Perhaps the most popular of the five blood lines descended from the Noriker was the Pinzgauer Noriker (now bred in Bavaria) mentioned above, improved by its breeders in the nineteenth century with Norman, Holstein, Hungarian, Oldenburg and Clydesdale blood.

220, 221 • Two fine examples of their breed, the **Rhenish Westphalian Draught** horse. Left: Eleven-year-old *Big Ben,* owned by Hans Biesenbach. Right: *Hurrican*, a six-year-old stallion from the regional stud farm in North-Rhine-Westphalia, led by the head groom Klaus Tönsfeuerborn.

223 • The *Tyrol Pesante Rapido* (**Italian** or **Rapid Heavy Draught**) the Italian cousin of the Noriker (from the Austrian side of the Tyrol) is worthy of its name ('heavy and fast'). It is fittingly represented here by *Nida*, a six-year-old mare shown by her owner Bortuzzo Natale.

225 • Magnificent in harness, the eight-year-old Austrian **Noriker** *Hercules*, presented by his owner Fritz Ehrensperger.

226, 227 • The northern horses. Left: *Marquis de Boehle*, a twelve-year-old **Belgian Heavy Draught** gelding, owned by Patrick Becker and presented by Céline Thelen. Right: *Inouïe d'Espérance*, a six-year-old **Trait du Nord** mare, owned by Lionel Corbier and presented by Michel Moreau.

Belgium: home of the draught horse

The saying 'no one is a prophet in his own land' could be applied to the Brabant (or Brabançon). Thanks to its particular characteristics and potent genes, this ancient breed, originally from the heart of Belgium, has contributed to the stock of most other European heavy breeds at some time or other, although it has now almost disappeared from its own country.

The Brabant has been sought-after for centuries by breeders from all parts of the world, and it has been crossed with mares throughout Europe and as far afield as Russia. The Shire, Clydesdale, Irish Draught, Trait du Nord, Suffolk Punch, Rhenish Heavy Draught and Ardennais are just some of the breeds that owe the Brabant a great deal.

The success of this powerful breed is due to the early establishment of its characteristics in the Middle Ages. Bred in Flanders and the Brabant, it was known at that time as the 'Flanders Horse'. Thanks to the heavy soil of these regions, it developed great flexibility in the knees, enabling it to pull its legs with ease out of the muddy morass into which the broad clay plains of the region descend when it rains. It was a trait that was carefully encouraged by the local breeders. At the end of the nineteenth century the classification of the breed was officially drawn up and sub-divided, with few variations, into three Brabant types: the large Gros de la Dendre with its light-bay coat, the Gris de Hainaut or Gris de Nivelles with a grey, roan or strawberry-roan coat, and the dark-bay Colosses de Méhaigne type.

These three breeds generally shared the same characteristics, which made them suitable for heavy agricultural or forestry work and all kinds of transport needs. They remain hardy and docile, stolid, tough, uncomplaining and undemanding. Their hauling power is immense and rivals that of the Shire. Today, the crossing of these three Brabant breeds is known as the Belgian Heavy Draught.

Certainly the Brabant – or Belgian Heavy Draught – is less lively than some of its rivals, to the extent that it could be described as phlegmatic, if not downright lethargic. Nevertheless, the Brabant and the many breeds to which it has contributed are much loved. Among them, the Trait du Nord deserves mention, cross-bred originally from two heavy-horse champions, the Ardennais and the Boulonnais.

In a report to the Equestrian Congress of 1912, Monsarrat, one of the founders of the breed's stud book, defined the Trait du Nord as 'an enlarged Ardennais, made fuller, taller and finer by the infusion of various blood lines. While it is undoubtedly true that in many aspects it resembles the Belgian horse … it is particularly distinguished by its refinement and energy.'

The extensive development of sugar-beet cultivation in the north of France, on the border with Belgium, played a considerable part in the birth of this new breed. The proximity of these two regions and their reliance on the heavy horse, led to the frequent exchanging of mares and stallions between the breeders of the two neighbouring countries.

On the French side, it was clear that powerful horses were needed, not only for the deep-ploughing of wet, heavy soil, but for pulling heavy loads of beet, stacked in wagons grossing five to seven metric tonnes in weight, to the sugar refineries at harvest time. Since the local French horses lacked the size and weight for this task, Belgian breeders were called in to help, and with great success – and so it was that the Trait du Nord continued the Brabant blood line but on French soil.

A fine example of the Trait du Nord stands 15.3–16.1 hh (160–165 cm), and by five years of age a stallion or gelding weighs around 900 kg (2,000 lb). The mares are hardy and solid and, even when in foal, can carry on working right up to the moment of giving birth without mother or foal coming to harm.

Of course, like all breeds the Trait du Nord does have its detractors. It has been called lethargic, a criticism that has been applied equally to the Brabant. However, it seems that although this was the case when the breed was first introduced, when the search for strength was paramount, from 1903 onwards the tendency towards lethargy began to be corrected.

Unfortunately, the two World Wars that ravaged the north of Europe and curbed cross-border relations were very damaging to both the Trait du Nord and its breeders – all the more so since a regular input of Belgian blood proved to be necessary to keep intact the breed's qualities, which tended to be weakened by the effects of the locality.

228 • *Bonar du Moulin*, a three-year-old **Ardennais** stallion, lovingly presented by his owner Céline Blaise.

229 • The three-year-old **Ardennais** stallion *Espoir des Joncs*, presented (with some difficulty) by his owner Pol Gonnet.

232, 233 • *Ludivine du Roseau*, a five-year-old **Trait du Nord** mare (by *Espoir de Bouvines* out of *Divine du Roseau*), owned by Claude Lemaire and presented by Bernard Bazelis.

The Ardennais: the perfect workhorse

If the Brabant appears as a kind of common grandfather to a number of European heavy-horse breeds, the Ardennais seems to be the Brabant's ancestor. After all, it can trace its ancestry (just as the Camargue, the Pottok and others besides them) to the Solutré horse, whose remains have been found in quantity at the base of the Solutré Cliff in Macon. The Ardennais takes its name from the Ardennes, the region adjoining the Franco-Belgian frontier, which is considered to be its true birthplace. The origins of its line stretch back to the Quaternary period and the creatures that lived in the Rhône, the Saône and the Meuse basins. One of the first horse breeds to be domesticated, its size and weight developed gradually over the ages. Archive documents reveal that by Roman times the Ardennais had made such a name for itself as a hard worker that Caesar's armies employed it too.

Much later, in the nineteenth century, breeders established its characteristics by gradually phasing out all crossing with animals from outside the region and only breeding from animals born and raised on home ground. Hailing from this large forested region in the south-east of Belgium that stretches into northern France and Luxembourg, the Ardennais has evolved into the splendid breed of heavy horse that we know today.

Its characteristics were determined by the climate originally – the long, cold, rainy and snowy winters of the Ardennes and the short but hot summers. As months of fine weather were relatively few and far between, the Ardennais was obliged to work very hard for most of the year, necessitating good health and a high level of fitness.

The rugged terrain that covered much of its territory, with its steep-sided hills and deep valleys, also played a part in the development of the breed, demanding great strength and energy. With an obedient and calm nature, the Ardennais became the perfect workhorse, ready to take on whatever tasks were demanded of it with skill and dexterity.

Physically, the Ardennais has a compact and muscular body, with an energetic and rather long gait, a strong head with an alert and friendly expression. It stands 15.1–16.1 hh (155–165 cm) and weighs about 900 kg (2,000 lb).

It is easy to understand why the military also made use of the Ardennais. It appears that in 1812, during the retreat by Napoleon's army from Russia, the Ardennais were the only horses able – albeit with great difficulty – to haul back to France some of the artillery and other heavy equipment. At the beginning of the nineteenth century, crossed with the Arab as well as the Boulonnais and the Percheron, the Ardennais gave rise to the three blood lines for which it is known today: the old type raised in the Vosges and Lorraine, and now very much reduced in numbers; the bloodline from the north known as the Trait du Nord, a strain made heavier by the addition of Brabant blood; and lastly the Auxois, a very heavy draught horse.

The Auxois: an unlikely racehorse?

You might think that, as with other breeds of heavy horse such as the Augeron, the Nivernais and the Trait du Maine, the Auxois line would have petered out slowly and quietly in the depths of its native territory in Burgundy, but in this instance you would be quite wrong.

Documents relating to the oldest racecourse in France are held in the municipal archives in Semur-en-Auxois on the Côte d'Or, the hillside region in Burgundy where many of France's finest wines are grown. According to local history, for years the townsfolk held an annual foot race at a large fair that took place in the town on the day after Pentecost. The winner received a pair of knitted hose, 'supplied by the shopkeepers and paid for by the guilds'.

On 16 June 1639, faced with the problem of attracting more custom for the fair, the town magistrates decided to organize a horse race in addition to the traditional foot race. By 1652 the winner's prize was 'a ring of gold to the value of fifteen pounds', the runner-up received a sash of white taffeta and the third a pair of gloves. And so the Course de la Bague (or 'Race of the Ring') was born.

Since then, with the exception of a short period between 1794 and 1804, when horses were requisitioned by the army, the race has been a yearly event, eventually moving to its present date of 31 May. In 2002, the Course de la Bague took place as usual, but this year there was a difference. The race had previously been run with saddle horses only, but in 2002 local heavy horses were included for the first time.

Burgundy, the native region of the Auxois, is considered one of the most beautiful and fertile in France, its rich soil providing abundant grazing for both Charolais beef cattle, a speciality of the region, and for the raising of sturdy foals.

The Auxois breed was the result of a cross between the Ardennais and a local horse, the old Bourguignon breed. Very little is known about the latter except that it was smaller and lighter than the line it helped to found and was used in harness as well as for work in the fields and woods.

As elsewhere, the Industrial Revolution that took place in the nineteenth century and the accompanying modernization of cultivation methods created the need for a heavier and more powerful horse. Today, the Auxois stands at 15.3–16.2 hh (160–168 cm) and has a coat that is normally bay or roan.

In 1913, the Auxois Horse Breeding Society (founded in 1900) succeeded in establishing a breed stud book, which they continue to promote today. And, in 1993, milk from Auxois mares was sold commercially for the first time. Apparently it is an excellent remedy for certain digestive ailments. Thankfully, rather than face the butcher's block, the Auxois continues to thrive today in its homeland.

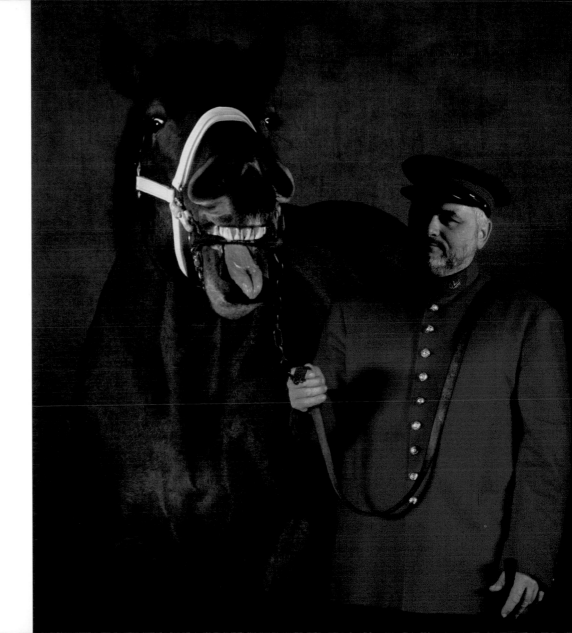

238 • *Koniz du Val*, a four-year-old **Auxois** brood mare, owned by Michel Petit
and presented by one of the principal organizers and backers of the Course de la Bague,
Michel Cortot (and his daughter Delphine).

239 • *Helena*, a seven-year-old **Auxois** brood mare, presented by her owner
Pierre Pasdermadjian.

241 • *Igloo*, a spirited six-year-old **Auxois** stallion, owned by the Cluny National Stud
and presented by Thierry Gallet.

243 • The seven-year-old **Auxois** brood mare, *Duchesse*, breed champion in 1997,
proudly presented by her owner Abel Bizouard.

The Boulonnais: a tough nut

The origins of the Boulonnais present something of a conundrum. Do its roots lie in a British breed, as some maintain? Did it ever come into contact with the horses of the Roman cavalry? What about the the old English black horse and/or the great horses of Northern Europe or the horses abandoned by Attila the Hun's army in the fifth century – have any of these contributed to the Boulonnais bloodline? How much do we really know about what happened to the Arab stallions and Barbs brought back from the Crusades in the eleventh century by French knights? There is even a certain amount of vagueness surrounding the first attempts at crossing the Boulonnais with stallions from Flanders. It was not until the beginning of the nineteenth century and the input of blood from Percheron stock that something about its lineage was finally recorded.

During the first half of the nineteenth century, the condition of the roads in the vast stretch of land between the Belgian frontier and the Seine Estuary at Le Havre was improved considerably, and the development of commerce and industry led to an increased need for road haulage. As a consequence, between 1830 and 1846 the amount of horse-drawn traffic on the roads doubled. The breeding of light coach/draught horses naturally followed the same upward trend.

The breeders set to work in all the areas of northern France that were active economically – specifically those around Boulogne, the wider Pas-de-Calais region that borders on Flanders, Picardy and Normandy and the area surrounding Paris. The nature of the land was in their favour: fertile soil generally rich in phosphates, beneficial for the development of strong bones, and plateaux of light, easily maintained soil that supports the abundant cultivation of crops. They could also draw upon the local people's long experience of working with horses at a time when oxen were used to plough the fields in other regions. In the north of France it was the Boulonnais mare that pulled the plough.

After a great deal of trial and error, including several attempts with Belgian stallions, the breed was finally improved, notably with input from Percheron stock. The final result was the Boulonnais. The horse we know today may not be exactly the same as the one first produced in the nineteenth century, but it is not too far removed. A graceful and balanced breed, the Boulonnais is considered a model of elegance. An average Boulonnais stands at around 15.3 hh (160 cm) and has a coat that is generally any shade of grey, from light to dark. Valued for its strength, in the past the Boulonnais proved its staying power by transporting fresh fish from Boulogne to the Parisian wholesale markets at a steady 16 km/h (10 mph) in the days long before motorized transport and railways. Since 1991, a bi-annual endurance race called La Route du Poisson ('The Fish Route') has been held, which retraces the original route and commemorates the sterling service that the Boulonnais gave to the French fish industry well over a hundred years ago.

The Comtois: a French favourite

Franche-Comté in the east of France, a mountainous region with a harsh climate, is home to the Comtois, a tough breed but active and sure-footed with plenty of energy and character. Much loved by its owners, its well-made legs with solid bones mark it out as a good workhorse.

In around 1905, a small Ardennais from Lorraine was selected as the best stallion with which to improve the local breed and raise its status to that of a true draught breed. The cross-breeding was a success and the Comtois stud book, opened in 1921, defined the breed in the following terms: 'Average size from 14.3 to 15.3 hh (150–160 cm), weight varying between 500 and 600 kg (1,100–1,300 lb), coat generally bay.'

Today, the breeding of the Comtois has been widely extended from its region of origin in the high Doubs to other mountainous regions, such as the Massif Central, the Pyrenees and the Alps. Whilst the Breton remains the most widely found heavy horse in France, the Comtois comes a close second.

251 • *Houblon*, an eight-year-old **Comtois**, (by *Duc* out of *Duchesse*), presented by Jean-Louis Cannelle.

253 • *Vivaldy*, a three-year-old **Postier Breton**, 950 kg (2,090 lb), presented by his breeder Pierre Hameury.

254 • *Kerenez de Kleg*, a three-year-old **Breton Draught**, presented by Jean-Luc Rauld.

255 • *Manvers*, a three-year-old **Postier Breton**, 850 kg (1,870 lb), breed champion at the Cordenas regional show in 2002.

Brittany: 'the mother of horses'

The day after the terrible storm of 15 October 1987, which ravaged Brittany and a large part of northern Europe, bulldozers were busy clearing the broken branches and trees brought down by the ferocious wind. However, due to the rocky nature of the terrain, the bulldozers were not able to penetrate off-road to clear away uprooted trees and vegetation. The obvious solution was to resort to traditional methods, so teams of Breton Heavy Draughts were made up, and the debris was soon cleared.

The love affair between Brittany and its native horse is long-standing. Thanks to tradition and a natural predilection for the animal, the Breton people are great horse lovers. There is many a tale that alludes to what could be viewed as a rather excessive attachment by some owners to their horses – those at Saint-Pol de Léon apparently kept them in their homes, fed them hot food and entrusted them to the protection of their local saint, Saint Eloy (Eligius).

There is also the story of a prisoner who was working on a farm in Germany during World War II. One day he was kicked by a horse and cursed loudly in the Breton language. The horse, although known for its bad temper, pricked up its ears and calmed down at once. From that day onwards, the horse was a reformed character, at least as far as the Breton was concerned – it would only obey commands from its compatriot in exile.

For centuries, the undulating and sometimes wild landscape of Brittany meant that the horse was the only possible means of transport. In the Middle Ages, the Breton peasants developed a breed of small but robust and compact horses that could be used both as riding horses and for carrying loads. The hard work in the fields was left to sturdy pairs of oxen, work to which they were better suited than the horses.

At the time there were numerous local types of the breed, but unfortunately the majority have disappeared over the years, as have, for example, the Trait du Cap, the Carrossier de Lannilis, the Criquet and the tiny Cheval d'Ouessant. However, the Bidet, a particularly sturdy and resilient strain of Breton, managed to survive. Centuries later, Napoleon – who called it 'the little Breton Cossack' – made great use of the Bidet in his cavalry.

Recently, breeders have developed two types of Breton breed: the Postier Breton, and the slightly heavier Breton Draught. Many attempts were made involving a number of different breeds before success was achieved – including crossing with Arab, Barb, Navarin and Limousin stallions, in an effort to inject some verve and distinction into the blood line of the local mares. Danish and Norman coach horses were also tried, followed by the Norfolk Roadster. A cross with the Hackney gave the breed its fine, high action and finally crosses with the Percheron, Boulonnais and Ardennais were also made. However, by the 1930s the breeders had given up on their attempts to introduce foreign blood into the stock.

Throughout the nineteenth and during the first half of the twentieth centuries, breeders were in a frenzy of activity. The story goes that, when the vets responsible for the horses working in the mines in various regions of France pointed out to the mine supervisors that they were tiring out their animals excessively, they always received the same response: 'The mother of the horses is not dead: Brittany will provide more of them....' They were right, and Brittany is still producing them today.

The Percheron: king of the heavy breeds

Which horse is deemed the archetype of all draught horses, the epitome of the breed and a point of reference for all breeders? It has to be the Percheron. Known throughout the world, its name has become synonymous with the heavy draught.

French in origin, its line has been enriched and improved by Eastern blood, to the extent that it has even been called 'an Arab breed'. There is a grain of truth in this, even if it did not happen exactly according to the legend. The story harks back to the battle of Poitiers, to the return from the Crusades of the Counts of Le Perche, and to incursions by the Norman Counts of Bellême into Spain. One thing at least is certain: it was during the eighteenth century and at the start of the nineteenth century that some new Arab strains were introduced to establish the characteristics of the Percheron, notably its famous dapple-grey coat.

In spite of the tales surrounding the origins of the Percheron, the fact remains that the local breeders knew perfectly well what they were doing. The quality of the local breeds, the expertise of the breeders and the effects of the terrain and the climate, which were manipulated skilfully, all played a large part in the success of this breed.

The relationship between horse and land has been mutually beneficial. The fertile and rich earth of the Orne, Sarthe, Loir-et-Cher and Eure-et-Loir regions has bred strong and powerful animals, while the land itself has profited from the hard work and legendary power of the Percheron. It is generally agreed that the breed began with *Jean-le-Blanc*, born around 1824 and sired by an Arab stallion belonging to the French national stud of Royal du Pin. *Jean-le-Blanc* lived to the advanced age of thirty-two and died with an unblemished record. An official from the stud farm said of him at the time: 'Although heavy and powerful, a true draught horse, there is something quite unique about his bearing. He possesses the characteristics of the breed so completely that people are inclined to take him for a large Arab.' This would seem to be an accurate judgment of this magnificent animal. It confirms that its working role has not impaired its development in any way – neither curbing its formidable energy, nor erasing the distinctiveness that is the result of its distinguished blood line.

Its success was predictable, and today the Percheron is the most popular heavy horse in the world. It has been exported across the continents, acclimatizing with ease to its surroundings and impressing everyone with its sense of contained power and attractive and noble bearing. It was way back in 1839 that the first Percheron was exported to the United States, where it remains very popular.

Percherons are as prolific as they are strong and healthy, and have given rise to other Percheron types. The Auge, Berry, Loire Nivernais, Bourbonnais and Maine are all descended from it. With its robust good health and generosity of character, the Percheron has come to represent the fertility and richness of the land from which it is bred. The hedges surrounding the pasture help to shelter it from cold winter winds, whilst it owes the solidity of its bones to the chalky soil of its homeland. It is thanks to the skill of the breeders that the Percheron can make such light work of heavy loads.

Percherons, with their grey or black coats, are patient and honest, docile and tireless workers, at times precocious but always gentle with children. They become part of the family, working willingly in partnership with their owners, many of whom come to regard their horses as inseparable companions and confidants that share their responsibilities, joys and sorrows, rather than beasts of burden. In the past, two distinct types were recognized: the Petit Taille or Postier, standing 15.1–15.3 hh (155–160 cm) with an average weight of 550 kg (1,200 lb), and the Grand (or Gros) Taille, weighing between 700 and 1,000 kg (1,550–2,200 lb) and standing 15.3–16.3 hh (160–170 cm). The former was generally used to pull mail coaches or vehicles delivering the post, whilst the latter was generally used as a draught horse.

Today, these types have been redefined. The Trait is a large horse, admired by the Japanese in particular. It weighs an average 900 kg (2,000 lb) and is suitable for agricultural work and haulage, while the Diligencier is more slender, lighter and highly valued for harness racing, as a rapid draught and saddle horse. The Americans are great fans of the breed, particularly of Diligenciers with black coats. Originally, as the name suggests, teams of four to eight Diligenciers pulled stagecoaches (*diligence* in French). The

heaviest of all horse-drawn vehicles, they weighed up to nine tons when fully loaded but were pulled along at a fast pace.

The French have a particular soft spot for the Percheron due to its long and illustrious career with the Paris Omnibus Company, which lasted from the mid-nineteenth century until 1913. At its peak, there were around fifteen thousand horses pulling heavily laden carriages – 1,700 kg (3,750 lb) when empty, much heavier when loaded with around thirty passengers – stopping and starting frequently along the set routes over the (often very slippery) cobblestones.

The Omnibus Company preferred to use grey Percherons with coats of as light a shade as possible to increase their visibility and limit the risk of collision – particularly in the evening when the light began to fail. Horses were just as prevalent on the cobblestones of the city therefore as they were in the fields of the countryside.

After many years of gruelling work trudging the streets, the time came to retire, and for the Percheron it was generally a return to the land. There, with a friendly farmer and his family, the horse could grow

old in peace, with the satisfaction of a job well done.

256–257 • The ten-year-old **Percheron** stallion *Gallien,* by *Silver Shadows Sheik* (US) (by *Lo Lynd Joc Lac*) out of *Toscane* (by *Neubourg*), owned by Sylvie Biget and presented by David Jollivet. *Gallien* has been at the Haras du Pin Stud Farm since 1997.

261 • An 'English' **Percheron**, *Three Holes Grenadier*, presented by his owner Richard Johnson.

262 • *Momino*, a three-year-old **Percheron** stallion (by *Éditeur* out of *Craminette*), presented by Michel Lepoivre.

263 • *Terrible*, a ten-year-old **Percheron** stallion (by *Iran* out of *Lorraine*), with his owner Michel Lepoivre (Saint-Aubin-de-Courteraie).

264 • The nine-year-old **Percheron** *Galopin Delanoe,* French national stallion (by *Quarte* out of *Voltige*), presented by Joseph Dudouit.

265 • The **Percheron** *Maître d'Atout*, held by Joseph Dudouit, and *Julie Sheik du Sap,* a six-year-old **Percheron** mare, held by Daniel Bourges.

Horse or pony?

While most breeds of large horse are the result of man's intervention through selective cross-breeding, ponies owe their existence and survival to themselves alone. Adaptable, robust and tough, in just fifty years ponies have seen their status improve beyond all measure. Instead of being exploited as beasts of burden, they are now the beloved playmates of many children, and today many horsemen and women fondly remember learning to ride on their very first pony.

The Icelandic horse: a true performer

All ponies can walk, trot, canter and gallop from the day that they are born. Icelandic horses can do even better, boasting two additional paces – *tölt* and *skeid* – which are both a kind of lateral gait that seems to come quite naturally to them. The *tölt* (or 'running walk') is a four-beat gait where one foot is always in contact with the ground, whilst the *skeid* (or 'flying pace') is a faster, two-beat gait.

Black, bay or grey, with a thick coat, bright eyes and small ears, the Icelandic horse has a complex ancestry, descended from Celtic ponies from all over northern Europe following the discovery of Iceland by the Vikings in AD 795. Less than two hundred years later, Iceland passed a law that forbade the introduction of any foreign animals into the country and, as a consequence, the Icelandic horse has evolved in a vacuum. Today, Icelandic law governing the movement of horses is very strict. No horse that leaves Iceland is allowed to return, even if, for example, it is simply to attend championships held in other European countries, where ponies from the Frozen North are now much in vogue. This strategy does have its disadvantages, however: the Icelandic horse is in need of new blood, and Germany is currently breeding some excellent Icelandic stallions.

Often raised in semi-liberty, the Icelandic horse is able to withstand extreme temperatures, surviving winter out in the fields. Never broken in before the age of five, it has shattered all records for equine longevity: the oldest recorded age is fifty-seven. Although standing only 13.2 hh (137 cm), Icelandic horses can easily carry adults, who enjoy the comfortable ride and are better equipped than children at channelling the exuberance to which these horses are sometimes prone. According to local legend, Icelanders became greatly attached to their horses because of their ponies' skill at finding their way home in the small hours, with their charges clinging unsteadily to their thick manes after a night's carousing!

Whilst able to boast little in the way of showjumping skills, Icelandic horses are no strangers to the dressage ring (where special events allow them to show off all their paces) and TREC or endurance riding courses (designed to test the qualities of horse and rider over an outdoor course), but they have been known to abandon these in favour of the racecourse. For the last one hundred and fifty years, races have been organized in Iceland in spring. The most famous of these takes place in Reykjavik on Whit Monday.

Ponies from the British Isles: equine royalty

Ireland, the Shetland Islands, Dartmoor, the Dales – in the British Isles the pony is king. Since the Bronze Age, the Shetland Islands, at the northern most extreme of the United Kingdom, have been home to the eponymous tiny pony beloved of small children and known throughout the pony club world in the West as a 'Sheltie' or 'Shet'. Often piebald in colour, with its thick mane and tail, soft, shaggy coat, large nostrils and 'double' (i.e. cleft) rump, it tends to rank second only to the teddy bear in terms of popularity among children. Independent and playful, though known to bite, it is, paradoxically, the strongest of all breeds in proportion to its size. Nothing fazes the Shetland – it can carry a man of 85 kg (13 stone) over 100 km (62 miles) or haul a laden wagon in the depths of a mine without losing its good humour. It excels at all equestrian disciplines and can boast that it has borne the showjumping champions of the Western world over their first jumps.

It is not known how this pony arrived in the Shetland Islands. Perhaps the Nordic ponies took advantage of the Ice Age to return to the tundra? Equally intriguing is its diminutive size – it rarely stands higher than 10 hh (100 cm). The harsh soil, the cold, the wind, the lack of trees and green fields undoubtedly form part of the explanation, and the Shetland pony sometimes had to eat seaweed in order to survive. It probably received an injection of Arab blood at some point during the Crusades and the medieval trade routes that opened up between Norway and the Shetland Islands almost certainly also influenced the pony's appearance.

The Connemara pony, on the other hand, has a much purer line. Until the arrival of the Celts, it had not been infiltrated by any foreign stock since the British Isles were formed some fifteen million years ago. The first cross-breeding produced the Irish Hobby, the ancestor of the Connemara, a horse so well loved and so much a part of Irish life that it even adorned a postage stamp. The only indigenous horse in the country, the Connemara still lives in semi-liberty in the far west of Ireland, in the lakeland region that bears its name.

At one time, every farm had a Connemara for cultivating the land, pulling the farm cart and ferrying the family about the countryside. According to the history books, it was in 1588, when the Spanish Armada was forced to disperse after failing to invade England, that a few Spanish ships were found to have drifted ashore along the Irish coast. Legend has it that the horses on board wooed and conquered some of the local mares, explaining the origins of the delicate features of the present-day Connemara. Originally dun with a dorsal (or eel) stripe and black mane and tail, it is now often grey, black, brown or bay.

By nature, the Connemara is the most well-balanced of all ponies and it is also the best showjumper. It excels at polo and has proven to be extremely adept at *haute école*. Consequently, the breed has had its fair share of stars. In 1935, *The Nugget* jumped 2.2 m (7ft 2 1/2 in) at the 'International Horse Show' in London, at the age of twenty-two, whilst *Dundrum*, who was only 14 hh (142 cm), cleared 2.13 m (7 ft). The extraordinary American *Marcus Aurelius*, a cross between Connemara and English Thoroughbred, won the gold medal at the Pan-American Games in 1976. Nor should we forget the incredible *Cannon Ball*, born in 1904, who won the local farmers' race in his region for an amazing sixteen years in a row. This horse travelled 100 km (62 miles) every week to take his master to market – mounting mares as he went. When he died in 1926, he was buried in a grave filled with hay, according to the Irish tradition.

279 • *Ted*, a seven-year-old **Connemara** stallion, used as a 'teaser' at the Gilltown Stud in County Kildare, Ireland.

281 • The fourteen-year-old **Connemara** stallion *Cyrano Pondi* (by *Galway de la Dive* out of *White Granite*), owned by Gilles le Mouellic.

282 • *Ulverscroft Sandstar*, a four-year-old **Shetland** pony, owned by Mrs P. V. Renwick (England) and presented by the Trott family.

283 • *Idole du Tregor*, a twelve-year-old 'French' **Shetland** brood mare, owned by Francis Glas (France) and presented by Pamela Mengy.

Scottish and Welsh ponies: hardy companions

The Welsh pony, the most famous of all British ponies, was very nearly wiped out on a royal whim. King Henry VIII (1491–1547) decided that he wanted to encourage the breeding of warhorses and ordered the slaughter of all mares under 13 hh (132 cm). However, some of the mares escaped by taking refuge in the Welsh Mountains and, thanks to some Arab stallions that had reverted to the wild after arriving with William the Conqueror five hundred years earlier, the elegant Welsh Mountain pony line was founded. Gentle, hardy and strong, this is the smallest of the Welsh ponies, standing at about 10 hh (100 cm). A skilful jumper and a good companion – although a little stubborn – the Welsh Mountain Pony is an excellent pony-club mount, ideal for children learning to ride.

There are many types of Welsh pony throughout the world, but only four kinds are listed in the stud book: the Welsh Mountain Pony; the Welsh pony (Section B), or Thoroughbred Welsh Pony; the Section C pony, or Welsh Pony of Cob Type; and the Welsh Cob. The Welsh pony (Section B) was formerly ridden by shepherds but is now used for sport. The Section C pony, standing between 12.3 and 14.1 hh (130–145 cm), is the strongest and can carry an adult. Tough and sure-footed, it is an ideal trekking or harness pony, doubtless pulling travellers' caravans with much greater willingness than the loads of slate it once transported in the quarries of North Wales. The Welsh Cob, the largest of the breed, which stands up to 15.2 hh (157 cm), also worked in the quarries and is a descendant of the ancient Pembrokeshire Welsh pony.

The Highland pony, meanwhile, can boast genes that stretch way back into the mists of time. As its name suggests, it comes from the Highlands of Scotland. Large, tough and strong, it is often grey or dun with zebra markings on its legs and sometimes a dorsal (or eel) stripe on the back. It is very sensible by nature and is often used as a riding-school or trekking pony. It does, however, have something of a nefarious past – before whisky distillation was made legal, Highland ponies made very efficient accomplices to smugglers, enabling them to make a quick getaway before the authorities arrived.

285 • James Jackson, from Glasgow (Scotland), presents his **Highland** pony *Cross Bred*, at the 'Horse of the Year Show 2001', held at Wembley Arena, London.

287 • *Jasper de Kergroix*, a five-year-old **Highland** stallion, presented by his owner Frederic Tamarin, at the 'Salon d'Agriculture de Paris', 2002.

288 • Young Maxwell Knife proudly presents *Cymran Petra*, his eight-year-old **Welsh** pony.

289 • Lauren Soanne, aged twelve, bravely presents *Tulira Robuck*, a six-year-old **Welsh** stallion.

Welsh, Dartmoor, Exmoor and New Forest ponies: a novice's dream

To the south of the Welsh hills and across the Bristol Channel lies Dartmoor in Devon, the wild stretch of moorland that lends its name to a charming little pony, now one of the most common to be found in riding schools. Standing no more than 12.2 hh (127 cm), with small ears and large eyes, Dartmoor ponies are delightful, and owners of mares can be reluctant to be separated from them, thus denying them their chance to have foals.

The Welsh Cob played a part in the renaissance of the Dales pony, also known as the 'little Friesian', due to its black coat and gait. It is thought that the first Dales ponies were produced at the time of the Roman occupation by crossing the Celtic ponies from the Yorkshire hills of the north-east of England with Dutch Friesians. In the seventeenth century, Fell ponies – then identical with the Dales but living on the western side of the Pennines – were used as packhorses in the lead mines. In the nineteenth century, Dales mares were mated with a Welsh Cob called *Comet*, famous for his victories in trotting races. All modern Dales ponies are descended from this line. During both World Wars, they were requisitioned by the army, and by 1955 only four fillies were registered in the stud book. Steps were taken to revive the breed, and there are now six hundred Dales ponies living in their birthplace.

The moorland of south-west England is home to the Exmoor pony. Legend has it that some Andalusian blood was added to the line, thanks to a mysterious and mythical dun-coloured horse that once roamed the area. Having fulfilled his role and improved one of the oldest pony breeds, *Katerfelto* was subsequently captured, although history does not say whether he was rewarded for his services. Exmoor ponies have all the qualities you could possibly wish for, although they are afraid of dogs.

Further east, a large tract of heath and woodland on the edge of Hampshire is home to a pony that was forced to witness a change to its habitat in the late eleventh century, when William the Conqueror organized the large-scale planting of trees, naming the area the 'New Forest'. This did not, however, prevent him from meeting an untimely death by falling off his horse. According to another legend, in the eighteenth century the father of *Eclipse*, one of the most famous English Thoroughbreds, covered a New Forest mare (though how this came about is unknown), bringing some pure blood to this placid, careful and gentle animal. Breeding stock and forest ponies still live in the wild on the heath in the New Forest. Long accustomed to the traffic that passes on the roads cut through the forest, they make solid and dependable mounts, ideal for novice riders.

291, 293 • Rosslayne Misty Blue, an eleven-year-old **Welsh** pony, ridden (on the left) by Harriet, daughter of the owner Mrs Jessop (England).

294 • *Epson de Kergroix*, a ten-year-old **Dartmoor** stallion owned by Frederic Tamarin (France) and presented by Fabien Bordet.

295 • *Townsend Breeze*, an eight-year-old **Fell** pony owned by Mrs Sweeney (England) and presented by her daughter Cara.

The Fjord: a lucky escape

To envisage the kind of pony that would have existed in the Ice Age, take a look at the Norwegian Fjord, an extremely robust pony whose line has remained essentially pure over the centuries. Besides its dun (characteristically cream or yellow) coat, it has a dorsal (or eel) stripe on its back similar to that of the Asian Tarpan, and remains just as it was in the Viking era, when it was ridden into battle.

Despite this longevity, the Fjord nearly died out as a result of some unlikely cross-breeding in the nineteenth century. There were attempts to make the Fjord first taller, and then fuller in girth, but the results were not very convincing. Fortunately, a few prudent breeders did hang on to their pure-bred Fjord ponies and were able to bring some order to the breed. Three lines of strong and elegant ponies now dominate it, the descendants of three stallions named *Njal*, *Kare* and *Baronen*.

Standing between 12.3 and 13.3 hh (130–140 cm), the Fjord can tackle all kinds of tasks quite happily and is especially suited to agricultural work in the areas of Norway in which it is impractical to use motorized vehicles. From working in harness to trick-riding and dressage, the Fjord is now found widely across Scandinavia and indeed the whole of Europe, and there are currently some fourteen thousand of these ponies worldwide. Since the Viking era, the tradition has been to keep their mane trimmed, as the epitome of 'Fjord style' is to cut the silvery outer mane short enough to allow the black centre stripe to show through, giving the illusion of an arched neck like that of a Spanish horse. The thick forelock, however, is left untouched.

297 • *Kafka du Camp* (by *Duc d'Ober* out of *Agathe du Moulin*), a four-year-old **Fjord** stallion, presented by his owner, Michel Bousseton (France).

299 • *Chanel* (by *Cato* out of *Bacardi*) a six-year-old **Franches-Montagnes** mare (already weighing 650 kg or 1,433 lb), presented by Richard Olivier.

The Haflinger and the Avelignese: impressive ancestry

An edelweiss encircling the letter 'H' is the famous emblem of the Haflinger, the new darling of the equestrian world. Its commercial success can apparently be attributed to just one man, an Austrian who was rescued from the cold by a Haflinger one bitter winter during World War II. Such was his gratitude that he decided to turn the Haflinger into a star. However, the Haflinger is more than just a simple mountain pony: although descended from a heavy Alpine horse and crossed with Asian horses, it can boast a great thoroughbred among its ancestors. In the nineteenth century, a mare from the area around the village of Hafling was introduced to an Arab stallion, *Folie*. *Folie* was the son of *El Bedavi*, who could also count a Tyrolean mare among his own ancestors. The Emperor Franz-Joseph was bowled over by the little pony with the blond mane and gentle eyes. Nowadays, the sure-footed Haflinger is found worldwide and is an excellent family pony, with its chestnut coat and flaxen mane and tail.

Until the age of four when schooling commences, Haflingers live in semi-liberty in the mountains of their birthplace in southern Austria. This upbringing seems to suit them well as they have been known to live into their forties. Their closest relative is the Avelignese, also a descendant of *Folie*. There are currently some twelve thousand Avelignese in north-eastern Italy, Sardinia and Sicily, where they tackle the steep slopes with amazing ease.

Able to withstand both the cold and the heat, Haflingers would certainly have made excellent auxiliary army horses. With this in mind, in 1984 the Indian army acquired five thousand Haflingers for its cavalry, but the venture was not successful and represents the only blip in the breed's illustrious history.

The Swiss, meanwhile, are very proud of their Franches-Montagnes. Every August for the last hundred years, some forty thousand people have attended the horse market and show in Saignelégier, north of Neuchâtel near the French border. Along with traditional displays, harness racing, bareback racing, steeplechases, plus a show with some three hundred horses, and prizes awarded to the local breeders' finest animals, the Franches-Montagnes, or Swiss Draught, is celebrated at these events to the full.

At the end of the nineteenth century, across Switzerland and most of Europe a war was waged between cross-breeding enthusiasts and advocates of strict selective breeding as to the best method to improve this horse. It resulted in the redefinition of the breed's region of origin and therefore a change in status from 'Swiss' to 'Jura' pony. To make matters worse, the Swiss army refused to have anything to do with the Franches-Montagnes and decided to use foreign horses instead. In 1987, the breeders organized the first Saignelégier horse market and show in response to this. Shortly afterwards, the establishment of a genealogical register for the breed finally introduced a degree of order into the breeders' activities, and the characteristics of the Franches-Montagnes were established. It can be any solid colour, dappled or roan but never white (or technically 'grey'), which is puzzling, given the number of inns in the region with 'White Horse' in their name! Standing between 14.3 and 15.3 hh (150–160 cm), with solid joints and hard legs, it is robust, sensible and docile. Used as a saddle and harness horse, it is both light and sturdy, a little more versatile than its French cousin, the Comtois, which lives on the other side of the River Doubs.

Well aware of the breed's fragile and uncertain future, Swiss breeders are attempting to export Franches-Montagnes, emphasizing their excellent nature and aptitude for working in harness.

301, 303 • Two Alpine cousins: page 301, *Miss Marriand'l*, a two-year-old **Haflinger** filly owned by Alain Buisson and page 303, *Efraim,* an **Avelignese** owned by the Italian forestry commission and presented by Massimo Scalacci.

Small horses from the Pyrenees: neglected talents

The Merens, the Castillon, the Ariégeois and the Landais are all breeds hailing from the South of France. Fairly small, with dark, or sometimes roan, coats, they often have hairy muzzles, useful when extracting food from prickly shrubs, and are closely related to the Pottok, whose name in Basque means 'small horse'.

Although now a single administrative region known as the Ariège, until recently Gascony and Languedoc had different cultures, languages and even sheep. It would therefore not be surprising if the horse breeds of the two regions did not differ too, albeit not greatly. Since there was very little communication between these isolated valleys, the breeds were able to retain their own characteristics. People from the region crossed frequently into the Pyrenees, so it is quite possible – as eminent French specialist, breeder and trainer Olivier Courthiade once said – that all the local horses have common Spanish ancestors. This is particularly true of the Navarin, which has now died out. Much prized by horsemen during the eighteenth century, it was somewhat similar to the present-day Pottok.

At a time when horses were only valued for their labour, farmers crossbred their animals according to their needs. This is why the Cerdagne horses, for example, which lived on a high plateaux of the eastern Pyrenees and were used for centuries by the military, eventually died out after being cross-bred with heavy horses. A similar misfortune befell the Landais pony, known as the *poney des pins* (or *lédon*), from the coastal region of the Landes, whose sole living representatives today belong to the family sired by the famous stallion *Jongleur*. His slender frame was passed over by traders at local fair, in favour of the larger Barthais ponies from the meadows around the Adour. Although never in the rankings in competition at the agricultural shows of the early 1970s, *Jongleur*, an excellent trotting horse, went on to have a dazzling career on the racecourse, thanks to his Parisian owner.

Breathing some new life into these brave, free horses was one of the hobby-horses, so to speak, of the conservation movement that grew up in the latter part of the twentieth century, with the aim of preserving the old breeds. Some enthusiasts even succeeded in introducing a stud book for the local types.

In 1955, there were fewer than two hundred Barthais ponies, whose blood line was, by then, much diluted. However, in 1967, with the addition of a little Arab blood and a touch of Welsh, the Landais stud book was born. Generally bay, black or dark brown, with a fine, square head, sound joints and a full tail that brushes the ground but is lifted when the Landais is moving, this pony also made a significant contribution to the stock of the French riding pony, established in 1969.

The Merens was the French trick-riding champion of 1999 and excels in harness. Its gentle nature also makes it ideal for use in horse therapy. A small village horse from the Ariège, it has conquered the whole of Europe in less than fifty years. Thirteen thousand years ago, if the Magdalenian paintings in the Niaux Caves are to be believed, the Merens was of average size, with a velvety black, shaggy coat and long whiskers. Since then, its penchant for eating oak leaves has refined its line, and today it cuts an elegant figure compared to the Castillon, a heavier horse from the Ariège.

One story goes that the Castillon originates from Greece, as does the traditional folk costume worn in the high valleys of Bethmale and Biros in the Ariège. In the sixteenth century, having made his fortune in Greece, a Frenchman by the name of Jouanissou is said to have returned to his birthplace, bringing with him Greek livestock (including goats and breeding mares) and cloth. On the other hand, some historians assert that the French King Francis I (1494–1547) was riding a horse from Biros at the Battle of Pavia, on the day he was captured by the Spanish. Nowadays, the Castillon is a good leisure horse, happy to go anywhere. Saved from extinction in the 1980s, its future is now assured – it was recognized as a pure breed by the French Ministry of Agriculture in 1996. With its black mane and tail, and chestnut coat, it bridges the gap between the Merens and the Tarbais, a horse that was greatly loved by the hussars.

The Pottok (pronounced 'pottiok'), perhaps the best-known of the breeds which the conservationists are trying to preserve and the subject of many books, films and scientific papers, at one time must have traversed Europe bearing the warriors of the Visigoths.

Over the years, it has become something of a cult horse for the conservationists and now plays a major role in eco-tourism. In Bidarray, in the French Basque country, the Pottok Centre organizes guided tours of the Pottok Pyrenean Reserve. Spread over four peaks – the Baigura, the Rhune, the Usu and the Hatza-Mendi – these Basque horses with their wide-set eyes and black hooves live in total freedom just as they have always done, and still look very much as their ancestors did. Unfortunately, the Basque peasants took better care of their sheep than of their horses, which – being unprofitable – were tolerated, but only just, and made to live on poor land. The Pottok's participation in local cultural life is only fairly recent but it has formed part of the local Basque cuisine for many years! Nowadays, however, they live much more peaceably than their Spanish alter ego, the Galician pony, which is still used for meat.

304 • *Kenobi de Garosse*, a four-year-old **Merens** stallion, owned by Mr Bury and presented by Pierre Germain.

305 • *Guirantos d'Aulus*, an **Ariégeois** horse presented by Sylvain Salamero.

309 • *Kazan des Vieilles*, a four-year-old **Castillon** stallion, owned by Marie-Claude Bernard and presented by Jean-Christophe Goedgebuer.

311 • *Judo*, a five-year-old **Pottok** stallion, owned by the Grands Joncs Marins Stud Farm (Normandy) and presented by Jacomina Daneels.

312 • *Viwa Cap de Bosc*, a five-year-old **Landais** mare, owned by Alain Frère and presented by Bérengère Zamora.

313 • The eleven-year-old **French saddle pony** stallion *Farceur des Contes*, owned by Michelle Davenet and presented by Véronique Magrin.

314, 315 • *Gayrlock de Touvent*, a fourteen-year-old **Henson** (by *Chanell d'Oueux* out of *Artemis de Henson*), owned by Michel Beaufils, and twelve-year-old Enya de Henson (by *Urus du Sehu* out of *Teriam de Henson*), owned by Michèle Lejeune. The result of a cross between mares from the Somme basin (France) and Fjord stallions (Norway), the **Henson** is a very versatile breed (used as a saddle horse, in harness or as a pack animal) and has only been registered as such since 2003.

The horse's cousins

With the horse unquestionably at its head, the large *Equidae* family comprises a number of species, including zebras and asses. Among this 'herd' of cousins, the donkey, the domesticated descendant of the African wild ass, is more closely related to the horse than any other species. In fact, they are so closely related that they can even be interbred. When a donkey stallion (jackass or jack) is mated with a horse mare the offspring produced is a mule.

The donkey

It may seem somewhat incongruous to find a section devoted to donkeys and mules in a work entitled *Horses*. As they belong to a different species, their inclusion cannot be justified from either a zootechnical or even an aesthetic point of view. They are included here because Yann Arthus-Bertrand loves donkeys and wanted to make them a part of his photographic tribute to the horse. At the same time, it was a good opportunity to present a case for the humble donkey, which, despite its long association with man as a beast of burden, should surely be given a place in this book alongside its illustrious cousins.

The large *Equidae* family to which the horse belongs comprises seven different species. The three main groups within the family are the horse, of which there are two species (*E. przewalskii*, *E. caballus* – the domestic horse), the zebra, of which there are three (*E. quagga*, *E. grevyi*, *E. zebra*), and the ass with two species (*E. asinus* – the donkey or African ass, *E. hemionus* – onager or Asiatic ass). The horse species is extraordinarily diverse, but some types of wild ass are either endangered – such as the onager, usually known by its local name (*kiang* in Tibet, *kulan* in Mongolia,

ghorkhar in India and Pakistan) – or extinct, such as the Syrian wild ass (*E. hemionus hemippus*). The donkey is the domesticated descendant of the African wild ass (*E. asinus*) and/or the Nubian ass (*E. asinus africanus*).

Employed as a beast of burden since as early as 4000 BC, the donkey is often associated with the biblical lands of the Near and Middle East. According to the well-known anecdote, the Egyptian queen Cleopatra (69–30 BC) preserved her legendary beauty by bathing regularly in wild ass's milk.

The ass's other – and more prestigious – claim to fame is that, along with the ox, it was one of the few animals to witness the birth of Christ and was the animal upon which Jesus chose to ride into Jerusalem.

Even so, the donkey's distinguished past was not taken into account when it first appeared in Europe, at an unspecified but early point in history. The poor creature became the victim of both physical and verbal abuse and an object of mockery and ridicule, with just one exception – it did earn respect for its prodigious sexual prowess and the exceptional size of the jack's reproductive organ.

Recent years have seen it acquire a new-found and more respectable status in developed countries, where it is no longer used to carry loads or pull carts. Here, donkeys have become ever more popular, especially where children are concerned, and their numbers have increased significantly over the past twenty years. Gone are the days when the donkey's large ears were a symbol of stubbornness and ignorance; instead, they have become an asset, adding to the appeal of an animal which is sometimes kept as a pet. Today, donkey foals can be bought at quite reasonable prices from the many donkey sanctuaries that have sprung up in rural Europe. In some cases, their owners – often unprepared for and sometimes disconcerted by their new pet's behaviour – have been obliged to turn them out to grass or simply use them as 'living lawn mowers' for the family's second home. Donkeys are also being used increasingly in the tourist industry, to carry walkers' backpacks on long-distance hikes, perhaps inspired by the Scottish writer Robert Louis Stevenson's (1850–94) account of his experiences in *Travels with a Donkey in the Cévennes* (1879).

Still, the donkey's improved lot in some parts of the world should not blind us to the fact that it is even more of an endangered species than certain breeds of horse and runs the risk of becoming extinct through lack of use. Overall, worldwide, the donkey population is on the decline, even in those countries (especially North Africa) in which it is still relatively widely used. This is a much more serious problem than it would first appear. It is not just a question of declining numbers; entire breeds are disappearing. For example, until relatively recently, each French region had its own 'breed' of donkey, so there was a wide variety in size – between 9.3 hh and 14.3 hh (100–150 cm), and even 15.3 hh (160 cm) – type, colour and aptitude. Today, only a few of these 'breeds' survive, with numbers in decline. For example, the Poitou (or Poitevin) and Pyrenean breeds number only around three hundred each.

The most picturesque is undoubtedly the Poitou, a large donkey standing between 13.3 hh and 15.1 hh (140–155 cm), with strong limbs and a thick, dark-bay coat. Its reputation is due not only to its striking shaggy and ungroomed appearance but to its quality as breeding stock – Poitou jacks are highly prized throughout the world for the production of mules.

316 • *Gamin*, a grey **Provençal donkey**, with his owners Roland et Marie Pevent.

321 • This pretty six-year-old **Poitou donkey** mare (440 kg/970 lb and 14 hh/142 cm) (by *Ultime* out of *Voleuse*), was French champion in 2003. She is owned by Jean-Pierre Mariot and presented by Céline and Emilie.

The mule

The mule is the result of an inter-species breeding, produced by crossing a horse mare with a donkey stallion. Surprisingly, the offspring of this pairing retains all the qualities yet none of the defects of its sire and dam. The mule is another example of man's creative ingenuity and our irrepressible desire to transform nature, adapting and controlling it for our own ends.

The mule would not be able to exist without man's intervention since there are no instances of natural coupling between different species, however closely related. The basic instincts of both horse and donkey have to be overcome in order to persuade them to participate in the reproductive act.

Attempts to cross different species in this way are by no means a recent phenomenon. It is reasonable to suppose that such attempts were made as long ago as the first domestication of these animals, and it is likely that many permutations were tried, although successful results may have been few and far between. In the cattle family (*Bovidae*), bulls have sometimes been successfully crossed with yaks (Mongolia) and, in the camel family (*Camelidae*), attempts have been made to cross Arabian camels or dromedaries with Bactrian camels (Turkey). However, it was in the horse family (*Equidae*) that these crosses were the most inventive, as can be seen from old documents referring to a hybrid that was produced by crossing a zebra with a donkey. Today, these zebra-donkey crosses (known as zedonks or zonkeys) are becoming increasingly popular, as is the zebra-horse cross (the zorse), the unlikely sounding cross produced by putting a zebra stallion to a horse mare. Attempts have also been made to cross horse stallions with donkey mares (jennies), but their offspring (the hinny) does not have the same qualities as the mule.

Calmer than the horse and more lively than the donkey, the mule lives longer than the former and is more active than the latter. Its sure-footedness makes it ideally suited to mountainous terrain, while its ability to carry heavy weights makes it an equally good pack and saddle animal. It is also enduring and, whether ridden or in harness, is ideal for covering long distances.

Today the mule, which was widely found and used in Ancient Mesopotamia, is still produced and worked in countries throughout the world. Mules have to be 'produced', crossing a good brood mare with a strong jack because, like all hybrids, mules are sterile. If the jack appears reluctant to perform, it is given verbal and, if necessary, manual encouragement. However, sterility is not synonymous with impotence and the virility of the males can be so excessive that, in certain countries, they are automatically castrated.

There is no established standard for mules: their size and colour depend on the choice of sire and dam, especially the dam. Although some breeds of mare are better suited to producing mules than others, in principle any breed can be used. Andalusian mares are used in Spain, Murgeses in Italy and Appaloosas in the United States. About twenty years ago, the Indian army acquired a job lot of Haflinger mares and a Poitou jack with a view to producing mules. According to Pyrenean breeder Olivier Courthiade, who puts Catalonian jacks to Breton mares, Thoroughbred mares were once widely used in mule production. He quotes the example of champion racehorse *Monsieur Piperlin*, winner of the Auteuil Steeple-Chase in 1901, whose half-brother was a mule.

The United States is now the only country in the world where a racehorse would be covered with a donkey. The Americans choose the breed of the dam according to the use to which her offspring are to be put. So, Thoroughbred brood mares are used to produce racing mules, Quarter Horse mares to produce sporting mules, and Percheron or Belgian Draught mares to produce draught mules.

In Europe, where the mule has for some reason never had a very good press, its use is declining dangerously. Fortunately, however, the reverse is happening in the United States, where mules enjoy a good reputation and are increasingly used in a wide variety of different areas. From racing and jumping to parades, *haute école*, rodeo and driving (singly, in pairs, or in teams of six or even twenty), mules seem able to adapt to most disciplines. Perhaps one day they will be used in polo matches, but they really come into their own in the field of endurance and, in events open to both mules and horses, it is not uncommon for the latter to be outperformed by their long-eared cousins.

In America's land of opportunity, some enterprising individuals have even created 'mule rental' businesses, which hire out pack mules to work on sites that are steeply sloping. Not only are they ideal for this type of terrain, they are also a cheap alternative to other means (such as helicopters) of bringing goods and materials onto these sites. It appears that the entrepreneurs have made quite a 'killing'.

325 • *Doly de Cadéac*, a four-year-old **Pyrenean mule** (by *Solide* out of *Venus de Cadéac*), is owned by the Ecole des Mulets (Nescus) and presented by Olivier Courthiade.

326 • *Kourout*, a four-year-old **Poitevin draught horse** (by *Coquelicot* out of *Aurore*), is owned and presented by Jean Clopes. The mares of this breed are sometimes used to produce mules.

327 • *Dolly*, a **Poitevin mule** (by *Lizeron*, a Poitou donkey, out of *Victoire*, a Poitevin mare), presented by her owner Jean Richard.

On the other side of the canvas…

'You've made the canvas too wet! It'll never dry!' The usual wave of panic swept through the camp before the shoot. The dripping canvas, still soaking wet, was suspended between two poles in the middle of a field in Montana. Everything had to be ready in less than an hour. The memory of this particular shoot at a riding school in France, struggling with a canvas still marked with damp patches, haunts Yann Arthus-Bertrand to this day. We had to resort to hiring a dryer to help us restore the canvas to its proper colour.

The canvas or tarpaulin was the key accessory in the travelling photographic studio assembled for each shoot. Wetting the canvas was essential. It was the only way the marks caused by folding it for transport could be erased. However, today, with the aid of the winds across the great American plains, there was no problem. It would be dry in a few minutes. Still, the wind itself presented difficulties, tugging at the canvas and making it fly up. The placid Quarter Horses were not at all disturbed by the flapping canvas, but the lighting equipment was blown over onto the grass, while the cowboys waiting patiently nearby laughed at us doing battle with the wind as we tried to secure the canvas to the ground. They finally came to our aid, resulting in a photo session that was a little more makeshift than we had planned.

In over fifteen countries, some of the most beautiful examples of the equine race have paraded in front of our canvas, or rather canvases. I say 'canvases' as, depending on the location, we set up what we termed a 'full studio' or used a canvas in a rather more makeshift fashion. The 'full studio' version, using a 10 x 10 m (33 x 33 ft) canvas weighing over 40 kg (88 lb) was used for shoots at horse shows. At the end of just a week of shooting at the shows, we would have an enormous collection of images of the finest representatives of the dozen or so breeds that usually attended them. Setting up the full studio version allowed Yann to get the lighting just right in order to create the atmosphere he wanted to achieve.

Holsteiner, pure-bred Spanish, Murgese, Maremmana, Arab-Berber – we drew up a list of the breeds present at each show to make sure none were missed. We then sought out the best of each breed and tried to persuade their owners to give up some of their valuable time during the busy show week. It was a risky business at times – when we tried to lead four gigantic Friesians to the 'studio' through the centre of a large crowd, for instance. Over the past fifteen years, the breeders at the 'Paris Agricultural Show' had become accustomed to Yann's presence and were quite happy to participate. The Russian breeders, however – to whom we tried to explain (in Russian) that we wanted them to pose with

their horses in our makeshift studio – were somewhat surprised and not a little suspicious. Less so than the British, however, who seemed to expect that they would have to pay for the photograph!

'The Maremmana has pulled out. The Avelignese is coming instead.' Françoise and Arnaud started to panic. Instead of the large black horse they were expecting next, a little horse with a dun coat was on the way. All the light settings would have to be changed. Luckily, Yann and Françoise have been working together ever since Yann started taking photographs of animals. 'Put the front lights at a lower angle, but not on the right, on the left…. I know what I mean … or at least Françoise knows what I mean!' Nearly one hour later and Françoise, tireless as ever, is still at it: 'Shall we try with the whole family next to the horse? What if we let the horse loose?' Everyone puts forward their ideas for giving the photo some life and tries to work out the best way for each horse to be positioned. A lifeless image would be useless.

The problem with the 'full' studio version was its sheer bulk. From the 'Paris Agricultural Show' to the 'Horse of the Year Show' at Wembley, or 'Equitana' in Essen, Germany, we managed to transport all the equipment in a camper van and horsebox. However, things became a little more complicated when the Russian

'Equiros' Show in Moscow began to loom: how could three people, each with 150 kg (330 lb) of luggage in metal trunks, avoid attracting the suspicion of the Russian customs officers? The Russians did not let us get away with it and confiscated the generators, light boxes and canvas at the airport! Four days of hellish negotiations, sleepless nights, and a dozen or so official letters from various people and organizations, and finally the customs officers, who in the end became sympathetic to our cause, received official authorization to release the equipment. The show was opening the next day. We had just one night in which to set up the studio in the barn we had rented, by torchlight. Suspended from beams more than 5 m (16 ft) above the ground, the canvas was fixed in place, with no distracting folds and just in time to capture the soulful eyes of an Akhal-Teke.

Like people, however, horses are an integral part of their surroundings, and confining an animal that symbolizes freedom indoors in order to take a photograph seems to lessen it in some way. On the other hand, the open air version of the studio – set up in the middle of the countryside – allowed us to convey much more fully the ambience of the life led by the horses and their riders, still, of course, with the canvas as a backdrop. The equipment for shooting outside was much lighter and less obtrusive: 150 kg (330 lb) comprising two solid camera stands, two battery-operated flash units and a smaller version of the canvas (6 x 3 m/20 x 10 ft). All we needed then was a long rod, sturdy enough to hold the canvas. 'In Cameroon we secured the canvas with ropes, didn't we?' But in Chile there were no trees. 'Bamboo won't hold up the canvas, it's not solid enough – what about the flagpole? Too heavy!' Each shoot was different and brought its own set of problems; we had to be flexible and adapt each time, making do with what was available.

Each outdoor shoot was like creating a *tableau vivant*, with the horse as the principal character against the canvas background. Sometimes, however, the composition became difficult to control, especially with twenty beaming Kyrgyz horsemen standing around the canvas at an altitude of 2,800 m (9,186 ft), with a herd of sheep, two eagles and rain threatening…. His eye pressed to the viewfinder, Yann took in the scene and assumed the role of director: 'Sheep to the left more. Eagle, turn your head towards me. Can't he beat his wings? The horse is lifeless – prick up your ears!…. This is terrible. The horse won't prick up its ears, the sheep have strayed off, the eagle's not looking the right way, the horsemen in the front row are hiding the others.' Total disaster and then, finally, the horse deigned to lift an ear, the horsemen managed to bring the sheep back, the flash bulbs synchronized and the camera worked its magic. 'Don't change a thing. That's wonderful!' (see pages 8–9).

We would often keep going until nightfall, when fading light would finally put an end to the shoot. For each successful image, dozens and dozens of compositions were tried out before finding the perfect pose. It was rare for everything to come together at the right time, so we would carry on until that magical moment took place…. As the equipment was packed away by torchlight, we tried to remember to collect every last piece, ensure the permission terms were signed, and take down as many details as possible about the horses and their owners, so that later we could accurately match up the images with the subjects. Not an easy task when it was already late at night and everyone was eager to get away at the end of the shoot.

When we explained to our friend Tota in Iceland that we shot from sunrise to nightfall, she chuckled: 'But here at this time of the year the sun doesn't really set!' Indeed, at two o'clock in the morning it was more like dusk when we finally decided to end the session for the day.

With racehorses, on the other hand, we had to be quick in order to catch them in front of the canvas between races. The number of these horses ready to pose in front of the canvas was limited. A racehorse needs to save its strength, just like an English Thoroughbred or a trotter! The mood or level of fatigue of the horse often meant we had to call it a day.

However, the concept of the outdoor studio often caused astonishment and did not convince everyone. The Kyrgyz, to whom we showed examples of previous outdoor photographs in order to explain what we wanted to do, smiled faintly: 'But where is the final photograph? You will remove the brown canvas for the real photo, won't you? It's not very attractive like that!'

We had the same reaction from a Frenchman who assisted us with our shoots in Qatar: 'Ah, I see you're well organized, you've got a canvas to protect you from the sun. But that must be difficult to remove on the computer!' The last two years of intensive photo shoots were also a technological turning point: we always used digital cameras when shooting at agricultural shows. Viewing the images on the computer screen, we could reach a verdict immediately: 'Too strong on the hindquarters! Lower the generators at the back – the spotlight settings on the canvas are not right.' The light settings could be checked immediately on the image, as could the position of the horse, the folds of the canvas, which all tended to push perfectionism to extremes. 'It's not bad but I think we can do better … let's carry on!' And so we carried on….

'What a shame we didn't go to Lipica for the Lipizzaners … and what about the Yakut horses? We'll go there this winter.' Just as a photo shoot is sometimes never quite finished, a book such as this – the stuff of dreams – will never truly be closed.

SIBYLLE D'ORGEVAL

Index of types and breeds of horses, ponies, donkeys and mules photographed

Index of types and breeds of horses, ponies, donkeys and mules referenced

Acknowledgments

I must first and foremost thank Sibylle d'Orgeval, who forced me to finish the book I began more than ten years ago. Without her contagious enthusiasm, her constructive criticism and, above all, her unbelievable energy, this book would not exist. Also Françoise Jacquot who, for the last fifteen years, has assisted me in my studio work with unfailing passion and friendship. I am very grateful to all the people who have participated in this worldwide equestrian adventure, in particular:

IN FRANCE:
The 'Salon International de l'Agriculture' ('International Agricultural Show') organization for many years of photo shoots; Mr Patria, President of CENECA, Mr Shaw, Chairman of the Comexpo Paris Executive Committee; Béatrice Collet, Director of the 'Salon International de l'Agriculture' and all her team, in particular Catherine Boillereau, Richard Redgen and Sophie Quiniou; Mr Vallogne, Mr Laroche, Pierrick David, the animal stewards, particularly Patrice Gourmaud, Dominique Jullien, Germain Breney, Jean-Luc Baudry, and of course Daniel Ygé; Véro and Gillou for their unfailing good humour, without forgetting Claude Lahaye and his assistant Jeanine Martinez-Munoz who authorized the first ever shoot at the show.
The organizers of the 'Foire Agricole de Lessay' ('Agricultural Fair'); Pierre del Porto from Sopexa and Alain Raveneau; Anne-Marie Capdaspe, Nelly Le Pautremat and Antoinette del Negro. Mario Luraschi and all his team, in particular Fadila and Joëlle Balland for their hospitality at the 'Ferme de la Chapelle', and for their wonderful professionalism.
The Haras Nationaux (National Stud Farms) headquarters: Les Bréviaires National Stud Farm; Didier Domerg and his team; Le Pin National Stud Farm, its Director Bernard Maurel, all his team, in particular Pascal Guimard, Vincent Juillet and Gilles Marnay. Jacinthe Giscard d'Estaing and the Triple Galop team; France Galop and especially Mattieu Vincent and Dominique

Gabel-Litny for their availability; L'AFASEC and Guy Bonnaventure Dominique Bœuf and Olivier Peslier; M. Baufils and the Association du Cheval Henson (ACH).
Mr and Mrs Katz for their invaluable help; Rodolphe Lacourte and Sebastian Pellon Maison; Mr and Mrs Guy Jonquères d'Oriola at Les Bréviaires.
The 'Société d'Encouragement du Cheval Français' ('Society for the Encouragement of French Horses'), in particular Isabelle Coltier and Caroline Freu; Océane Andrieu.
The Grosbois Training Centre; Sylvain and Michel Devulder; Christophe Walazyc; Mr Compiègne.
Virginie Bruneau; Jean-Paul Guerlain; Arsène Ronsé; Ms Flauder.

IN AFRICA:
Christian Seignobos and Gérard Roso for their invaluable knowledge of the country and being available to help us; His Excellency Mr Jacques Courbin, French Ambassador to Chad; the Embassy services, in particular Ms Chevalier, Mr Yann Apert, cultural consul.
Thierry Miallier from RJM Aviation in N'Djamena for his hospitality; ASF and their pilots, Guy Bardet and Bruno Callabat; Evelyne Payen at the Relais de la Porte Mayo (Maroua, Northern Cameroon); Fagus Voyages.

IN GERMANY:
The organizers of the 'Equitana Show' in Essen, Reed Exhibitions, in particular Nathalie Bondetti and Ana Lena Grytz; Geneviève Teegler from Géo Allemagne for translating.

IN ARGENTINA:
Jean-Louis Larivière; the members of the Sociedad Rural Argentina (Argentinian Rural Society) and their President Enrique Crotto; Mr Carlos Videla; Aerolinas Argentinas; Colette Larivière, Josefina and Ricardo Matho Garat from the 'Estrella' and Sara, Susana and Emilio Jorge Ferro from La Adela). Ignacio Corti Maderna; Enrique Baserga; Charles de Ganay; Augusto Salvo; Dudu von Thielmann; Mariano G. Fernandez Alt;

Antoinette Huffman; Mercedes Villegas de Larivière; Marina Larivière; Enrique Baserga.

IN BELGIUM:
Rodrigo Pessoa and his team at the Haras de Ligny Stud Farm for their Brazilian good humour.

IN CHILE:
Véronica Besnier; Lucho Weinstein; Italo Zunino for his hospitality and his 'pisco sour'; all the staff at the San Lorenzo farm.

IN SPAIN:
Don Angel Peralta, Don Rafael Peralta, Immaculada and the team at El Rocio ranch in Puebla del Rio; La Real Maestranza de Caballeria de Sevilla (Royal Order of Chivalry of Seville) for the photographs taken in the Seville bullring; Maria Jesus Buitrago Sivianes.
The Hierro del Bocado breeding farm in Jerez de la Frontera and the farm's blacksmith; the Chartreux monastery in Jerez de la Frontera, Sister Corinne and Don Alfonso Pacheco; Carmen Garcia and Lunwerg Editores; André Viard for his advice; Christina Heeren for her flamenco.

IN GREAT BRITAIN:
The organizers of the Wembley 'Horse of the Year Show', in particular Mike Gill and Clare Duncan; Philippe Achache for his friendship and invaluable help, plus his son George; Rosalind Mazzawi; the Royal Agricultural Society (RASE) Organizing Committee, the Royal Show and particularly Miss E. S. Binions (Royal Show Livestock Executive).

IN INDIA:
The French Embassy in India; the Indian government; the Indian Presidential Guard.

IN IRELAND:
His Highness Prince Aga Khan; Pat Downes, Director of the Irish Stud Farms; Julie White, Camilla Milbank and all the team. Peter O'Dwyer and Gisèle Scanlon.

IN ICELAND:
Gisli and Bergur Gislason; Thorunn Lara Thorarinsdottir (Tota)

and family, at Laxnes Farm, and Siggi; Ernir Snorrason; Heistheimar Stud Farm and Asta Begga, Gisli; the organizers of the 'Quinzaine Islandaise' ('Icelandic Event') in France, Chérif Khaznadar, Commissioner-General for France and Director of the Maison des Cultures du Monde (World Cultures Centre) and the Icelandic Commissioner Mr Sveinneinarsson; Stine, Soren, Franck and their energetic team!

IN ITALY:
Associazione Italiana Allevatori (Italian Breeder's Association) in Rome, its Director-General Fortunato Tirelli; Andrea Guiliani and the Verona 'Fieragricola' ('Agricultural Fair') Organizing Committee.

IN KYRGYZSTAN:
Jacqueline Ripart for her unique knowledge of Kyrgyz horses; Rash, his family and Shepherd's Way Trekking; René Cagnat; Idil and Ms Nessrin from Turkish Airlines.

IN LEBANON:
Lucien George, Georges Salem; Nabil Nasrallah and the team from Beirut racecourse.

IN MONGOLIA:
Gaëlle Lacaze; Sanduijav Altantuya, known as 'Tuyya' and her husband, Badraa Battulga and the Mongolie Voyages travel agency, His Excellency Mr Jacques-Olivier Manent, French Ambassador to Mongolia, His Excellency Mr Gotovdjorjiin Louzan, Mongolian Ambassador to France, the Mongolian Embassy in France, Mr Bayalag Erdem Gonchig, cultural attaché; Mr Schiilegdamba and Mr Bat-Erdene from the Mongolian Tourism Board.

IN QATAR:
His Highness the Emir of Qatar Sheikh Hamad Bin Khalifa Al-Thani; Sheikh Hamad bin Ali Al Thani, Director of the Al Shaqab Stud Farm, Willy Oppen and the team at the Al Shaqab Stud Farm; the French Embassy in Qatar, particularly Gilles Maareck.

Mr Hamid Abdelamid, Director of the Royal Bouznika Stud Farm (Morocco); Dominique Laubarie; Mr Richardot de Choisey; the Roissy (Charles de Gaulle airport, Paris) customs officers for their patience.

IN RUSSIA:
Nicolas Bordovskikh; the organizers of the Russian Horse Show 'Equiros' at the Sokolniki Exhibition Centre in Moscow and in particular the Director Liubov Arkhipova; Alexandre Kvasnikov; Gloria Raad; Olga Siblova; Oleg Gourev; Henrik Holten Hansen; Dinara Bakirova; the French Embassy services in Moscow, the customs officers at Cheremitiévo airport; Irina and Philippe for translating.

IN SENEGAL:
Sindiély Wade; the Senegalese Red Guard and Captain Djiby Tine; General Pathé Seck, High Commander of the Police Force and Director of Military Justice; Jean Poderos, the most African member of the Altitude team.

IN THE UNITED STATES:
William Kriegel for his hospitality and contagious enthusiasm; all the team at the La Cense Montana ranch and the La Cense de Rochefort-en-Yvelines Stud Farm; Jean Pierre Vergnier; Lisa Daguett.
Curly Bear Wagner; Bob Black Bull, founder of the Blackfeet Buffalo Horse Coalition.

I ALSO WISH TO THANK:
My successive assistants over many years of shoots: Fabien Dorio, Olivier Jeannin, Eric Lafitte, Denis Lardat, Marc Lavaud, Franck Lechenet, Dominique Llorens, Ambre Mayen, Jean-Philippe Piter, Olivier Pollet, Arnaud Prade, Jean-Paul Thomas. François Drion, breeder of champions…!
Air France, in particular François Brousse and Dominique Gimet, thanks to whom the equipment has been transported to some fifteen countries.

Janjac, in particular Olivier Bigot, Eric Macé, Erwan Sourget, Frédéric Gueguen, Thierry Vançon, Olivier Caron, Hervé Bollard and Eric Thillier for their sleepless nights.
The team at Editions du Chêne, in particular Joan Le Boru, Philippe Pierrelée and Isabelle Jendron; the Chine studio, Marc Walter and Sabine Arqué.
Lumiphot (Godard Flashes), and especially Gérard Devaucoux for his invaluable technical assistance; Jipe Labo (Norman Flashes), especially Alexandra; Avis-Car Away in Rueil-Malmaison, particularly Philippe and Isabelle Gueugnier; Le Ronchay weaving mill in Luneray for making our canvases, and Sylvie Mitot; the team at Fujifilm France, in particular Marc Héraud and Anissa; Canon, especially Guy d'Assonville, Bernard Thomas and Raphaël; Pentax, Éric Denoulay and Marc Albuisson; Shop Photo Prony; Pierre Peres Insurance, particularly Émilie; Emmanuel Perrault (eperrault@wanadoo.fr) who sent us the photograph on page 334.

A list of acknowledgments is never complete! Double thanks to anyone I have forgotten.

Y. A.-B.

328 • The canvas is not something we invented! It has been used in horse portraits since the earliest days of photography.

On the cover:
Front: *Flamenco*, a seven-year-old **Palomino** horse owned by Christine de Dorken (Divonnes-les-Basins/France).
Back: A **Mongolian** presented by Mr Enkhree and his seven-year-old son Bat-Erdenne, winners of a Naadam organized in September 2002 in the Khan Khenti region near Mongon Moor ('silver horse'), at an altitude of 1,800 m (5,905 ft).

Translated from the French *Chevaux* by Wendy Allatson, Sue Rose, Barbara Souter and Lydia Smith for JMS Books LLP.

First published in larger format in the United Kingdom in 2004
by Thames & Hudson Ltd,
181A High Holborn, London WC1V 7QX

www.thamesandhudson.com

Original edition, *Chevaux*, written by Jean-Louis Gouraud, with photographs by Yann Arthus-Bertrand © 2003 Éditions du Chêne – Hachette-livre, Paris

Reduced format edition © 2007 Éditions du Chêne – Hachette-livre, Paris
English edition © 2004 and 2007 Thames & Hudson Ltd, London

British Library Cataloguing-in-Publication Data
A catalogue record for this book is available from the British Library

ISBN 978-0-500-54353-5

Printed in China by Midas Printing Ltd